ATTILIO BERTOLUCCI
SELECTED POEMS

ATTILIO BERTOLUCCI

Selected
POEMS

TRANSLATED BY
CHARLES TOMLINSON

BLOODAXE BOOKS

ISBN: 1 85224 242 6

First published 1993 by
Bloodaxe Books Ltd,
P.O. Box 1SN,
Newcastle upon Tyne NE99 1SN.

Bloodaxe Books Ltd acknowledges
the financial assistance of Northern Arts.

ACKNOWLEDGEMENTS
Acknowledgements are due to the Arts Council
for providing a translation grant for this book,
and many thanks also to Hugh Shankland for his invaluable advice.
The Italian poems are reprinted from Attilio Bertolucci: *Le Poesie* (1990),
La camera da letto (1988) and *Verso le sorgenti del Cinghio* (1993),
all published by Garzanti Editore s.p.a., Milano.

Cover printing by J. Thomson Colour Printers Ltd, Glasgow.

Printed in Great Britain by
Bell & Bain Limited, Glasgow, Scotland.

To Ninetta and Brenda

INDICE

CONTENTS

ACKNOWLEDGEMENTS

Acknowledgements are due to the following for their publication or broadcasting of some of these translations: the BBC, *Agenda*, *London Magazine*, *Paris Review*, *PN Review*, *Poems from Italy* and *TriQuarterly*. I am grateful to the Rockefeller Study Center at Bellagio for time spent there while working on this book. A further debt of gratitude is due to Hugh Shankland who read the manuscript and suggested a number of valuable revisions. CT

INTRODUCTION

More than once, in reading the poetry of Attilio Bertolucci, I have thought of a passage from the Varykino episode of *Doctor Zhivago*. Yury Zhivago, thrown back on himself and his immediate surroundings in a country in chaos, begins to keep a diary. In this he writes: 'The words "bourgeois" and "middle class" have become terms of abuse nowadays, but Pushkin forestalled criticism in his *Family Tree*: "A bourgeois, a bourgeois is what I am"...' And then, later on, he says of Pushkin and of Chekhov: '... they live their lives quietly, treating both their lives and their work as private, individual matters, of no concern to anyone else. And these individual things have since become of concern to all, their work has ripened of it-self, like apples picked green from the trees, and has increasingly matured in sense and sweetness.' These reflections fit both Berto-lucci's origins and his art. The circumstances that gave rise to Zhivago's words parallel those of Italy in chaos in 1943, and the flight of Attilio, Ninetta and their son Bernardo, setting out on foot for the mountain village of Casarola – an event celebrated in a splendid poem, 'Towards Casarola'. That adventure of individuals now belongs to us all, with other poems nourished from deep family fidelities and tasting of the locality of Casarola and Parma. The poems tell the whole story in a personal manner far from the merely confessional. There is also a fascinating prose account of Bertolucci's life and literary affiliations, *I giorni di un poeta* (The Days of a Poet, 1980). This takes the form of a series of interviews, or rather a question is proposed and Bertolucci responds to it with an entire chapter. The whole manuscript was lost in a taxi in Rome and then miraculously recovered. It is to this volume that I am indebted for much of what follows.

Born in the neighbourhood of San Lazzaro, Parma, on 18 November 1911, Bertolucci was brought up in the country outside Parma itself, at what he calls 'the right distance from the "petite capitale d'autrefois"' – for the Bourbons and Marie Louise of Austria once ruled over that region. Parma and its domes and towers lay near at hand and their image has stayed with Bertolucci in the Roman apartment where he now lives – itself a reminder of that 'petite capitale', with its Parmesan furniture behind the unforth-coming façade of a modernish block of flats.

'I am,' he says, 'the son of an agrarian middle-class family.' His father came from the Catholic, upper but poor middle-class, consisting of landowners with scanty estates in the mountains; his mother from the rich, pagan middle-class of the contrasting valley of the lower Po. His problem was always to find a certain balance between these opposite extremes, but the blend has proved to be positive for him. He attended the Maria Luigia boarding school in his primary years and then high schools in Parma where, for a period, he also registered at the Faculty of Law, though with little profit.

In Bologna, he was a student of art history, passionately following the lectures of Roberto Longhi, and graduated from that university. 1951 saw his removal to Rome, but he kept a house on the outskirts of Parma and then in the mountains at Casarola – the stone house that had belonged to the Bertolucci family since the seventeenth century when they moved from Tuscany to Emilia 'with their horses'.

Bertolucci developed young. His first book of poems, *Sirio*, appeared in 1929 when he was only eighteen; his second, *Fuochi in novembre* (1934), was recognised and favourably reviewed by Eugenio Montale. A silence, which can surely only be compared to that of the American poet George Oppen (the causes were different and are hinted at in 'Ritratto di uomo malato' [Portrait of a Sick Man]), ensued until the appearance in 1951 of *La capanna indiana* which received the Viareggio Prize. Another period of apparent silence – a sign that Bertolucci was at work on his novel in verse – and then, in 1971, appeared *Viaggio d'inverno*, Bertolucci's most mature book to date and his most boldly experimental, with its roving syntax and its ability, in poems often centred on the family, to register the existence of 'what is happening over there', of a contingent and extending world which contains, nourishes and yet resists the poet. You seldom suspect at the beginning of one of these later poems where it is going to end. Indeed, Bertolucci's skill in frustrating the reader's anticipations of a likely closure is aesthetically the source of one of our most pleasing sensations as we travel with him through a poem.

A frequent cause of pleasure and also disquiet is Bertolucci's sense of time, the calm fire of the days. The tenor and the dependability of domestic life are both supported and menaced by this fire. Paolo Lagazzi in an excellent account of the poetry in his selection *Al fuoco calmo dei giorni* (By the Calm Fire of the Days, 1991), speaks of the poet, although slowly bleeding to death because wounded by time, as also drawing from time 'all the gifts, colours, sweetnesses still possible – while darkness and winter advance without truce'. Another Italian critic, Pietro Citati, writing twenty years earlier on the appearance of *Viaggio d'inverno*, could already say: 'Among the poets who are writing in Italy today, perhaps no one understands like him the art of breaking a line, of inverting a construction... [and] that binding together and loosening rhythms is the poet's chief duty.' I have tried to bring over some of these effects into English, even at the expense of stretching a little the seams of the language. The intricacy and tension of Bertolucci's work are all the more telling for the way they sound out the reaches of the ordinary – what you and I might feel in the course of a day though failing to take its due measure, allowing our own awareness to blur and thus forfeit the counterpoint and exfoliating richness of common experience. Italy is a land of inscriptions carved in stone. The last thing one feels about Bertolucci's verse is its suitability for a *lapide* – there is always something left over, something you cannot tidy away into epigram or aphorism and this is often exemplified by that closing single line of a poem in quatrains that insists on breaking out of the fold.

In the story of Italian poetry, Bertolucci signals the end of those symbolist ambitions transmitted until quite late on from Mallarmé and the French. The search for some kind of absolute poem is over. Irony has brought down that flight beyond the world of phenomena and place. He has read Montale and Eliot, but his world, unlike theirs, balances subjectivity and psychological unease against the presence of locality and his immediate family (what poet ever addressed so many poems to his wife and children?). In the young Bertolucci – in poems written between the age of fifteen and his early twenties – one can hear the tones of Apollinaire and Verlaine and also the more intimate side of d'Annunzio, even Ungaretti and Cardarelli. But listing names like these last three for an English reader is a somewhat academic exercise: a knowledge of Italian poetry is rare these days. It would be more intelligible to point to the Proustian element in his poems – the evocation of things past, the fluidity of time, the long sentences. English poetry has meant much to Bertolucci and his Proustianism seems to mingle with his high regard for Thomas Hardy, eight of whose poems he translated together with four of Edward Thomas. Indeed, 'Fragment' (p. 73) reads like an Italian version of Hardy's 'Neutral Tones', concluding with sentiments that recall the end of Thomas' 'October': '...who knows? / Some day I shall think this is a happy day.' And time and again the shape of Bertolucci's phrases, taking us we do not quite know where, puts us in mind of those of Thomas. Bertolucci also made an excellent translation of Pound's 'The Gipsy', a poem written during the latter's Imagist phase, and many of the Italian poet's earliest pieces are charming examples of Imagist modes. Lagazzi interestingly points to the influence of the short stories of Katherine Mansfield on the emerging forms of Bertolucci's verse. Before writing *La capanna indiana* he had translated Wordsworth, and Wordsworth's presence, de-transcendentalised, informs the account of childhood anxieties in 'How Anxiety is Born' (p. 133) from his novel in verse, *La camera da letto*.

The first volume of this ambitious work, begun in 1955, appeared in 1984, reaching its second volume in 1988. It is a kind of fore-shortened history of his family, particularly of his parents, his own childhood and his love for Ninetta Giovanardi, the mother of Bernardo and Giuseppe, his two film-director sons. Bertolucci says of *La camera da letto*, 'I do not dare to call it a poem, but perhaps only a novel in verse, with Pushkin's supreme example, *Eugene Onegin*, in mind, as well as some of the admirable achievements of Robert Browning.' It was the challenge of Poe's unduly famous essay 'The Philosophy of Composition', with its negation of the possibility of the long poem, and thus of the novel in verse itself, that put Bertolucci on his mettle in the wake of Baudelaire, Mallarmé and the death of that *symbolisme* which had deemed Poe so important. 'I am aware,' says Bertolucci, 'of the danger such an undertaking involves – principally a slackening of tension and even a drop into prose. But wouldn't it be worth it, I asked myself, to forego safer and more foreseeable achievements like the short poem, for the upper reaches made possible by a longer composition, a gradual approach to – who knows? – wholly unpredictable vantages and vistas?'

The success ('an unpleasant word,' Bertolucci has said) of *La camera da letto* among a wide audience that does not usually read poetry, as well as among those who do, has rapidly repaid his circumspect daring. The book is autobiographical, but the author speaks about himself only in the third person. He has likened this

14

to a painter, working on a self-portrait, and portraying a 'different' self in the painting as he stands in the flesh before it. His attitude to poetic language is (in the formulation of Hopkins, another English poet whom he admires) that it should be 'common language intensified'. How closely this approaches the words of Pasternak in the episode with which we began when, through Yury Zhivago, he stated, 'The fabulous is never anything but the commonplace touched by the hand of genius.' That Pushkin should have been both in *his* mind and in that of Bertolucci points perhaps to the revival of a form, the novel in verse, that had been prematurely buried under the weight of all those indifferent novels in prose that pour from the presses and receive such a disproportionate amount of attention in the reviews. Perhaps we should be suspicious of the bourgeois after all. The middle classes have been afraid of poetry too long. In Italy they seem to be re-awakening, confronted by this remarkable work which has made its way despite the public diffidence of its author.

CHARLES TOMLINSON

SIRIO
SIRIUS
(1929)

Vento

Come un lupo è il vento
Che cala dai monti al piano,
Corica nei campi il grano
Ovunque passa è sgomento.

Fischia nei mattini chiari
Illuminando case e orizzonti,
Sconvolge l'acqua nelle fonti
Caccia gli uomini ai ripari.

Poi, stanco s'addormenta e uno stupore
Prende le cose, come dopo l'amore.

Wind

It is like a wolf, the wind
That descends from the hills onto the plain,
In the fields it lays flat the grain,
Wherever it goes leaving dismay behind.

It whistles when mornings are clear
Lighting up houses and skyline,
It dishevels the water in the fountain,
Chases men indoors to the fire.

Then, weary, it falls asleep and a stupor
Takes all things, as after making love.

Mattino d'autunno

Un pallido sole che scotta
Come se avesse la febbre
E fa sternutire quando
La gioia d'esser giovani
E di passeggiare di mattina
Per i viali quasi deserti
È al colmo, illumina l'erba
Bagnata e la facciata rosa
Di un palazzo. Tutto è gioviale
Buongiorno e sereno, raffreddore
E mezzastagione. E Goethe
In mezzo alla piazza sorride.

Autumn Morning

A pallid sun that burns
As if it had a fever
And makes me sneeze when
The joy of being young
And of walking in the morning
Down the almost deserted avenues
Is at the full: it illuminates
The wet grass and the pink of façade
Of a building. Everything is one jovial
Good-morning and serene – cold in the head
And the off-season. And Goethe
In the middle of the square is smiling.

Torrente

Spumeggiante, fredda
Fiorita acqua dei torrenti,
Un incanto mi dai
Che più bello non conobbi mai;
Il tuo rumore mi fa sordo,
Nascono echi nel mio cuore.
Ove sono? fra grandi massi
Arrugginiti, alberi, selve
Percorse da ombrosi sentieri?
Il sole mi fa un po' sudare,
Mi dora. Oh, questo rumore tranquillo
Questa solitudine.
E quel mulino che si vede e non si vede
Fra i castagni, abbandonato.
Mi sento stanco, felice
Come una nuvola o un albero bagnato.

Torrent

Foaming, chill
Florid water of the torrents,
You set on me a spell –
I never knew one more beautiful;
Your din deafens me,
Echoes awake within.
Where am I? among great
Rust-red boulders, trees, woods
Crossed by shadowy paths?
The sun makes me sweat a little.
It gilds me. Oh, this tranquil sound,
This solitude.
And that mill one sees and then does not see
Among the chestnut trees, abandoned.
I feel tired out, content
As a cloud or a rain-drenched tree.

Solitudine

Io sono solo
Il fiume è grande e canta
Chi c'è di là?
Pesto gramigne bruciacchiate.

Tutte le ore sono uguali
Per chi cammina
Senza perché
Presso l'acqua che canta.

Non una barca
Solca i flutti grigi
Che come giganti placati
Passano davanti ai miei occhi
Cantando.

Nessuno.

Solitude

I am alone
The river is full and singing
Who is it over there?
I trample the scorched grass.

All the hours are the same
For someone walking
Without aim
Beside water that is singing.

Not a boat
Furrows the grey waves
That like placated giants
Pass in front of my eyes
Singing.

No one.

FUOCHI IN NOVEMBRE
FIRES IN NOVEMBER

(1934)

Fuochi in novembre

Bruciano della gramigna
nei campi
un'allegra fiamma suscitano
e un fumo brontolone.
La bianca nebbia si rifugia
fra le gaggìe
ma il fumo lento si avvicina
non la lascia stare.
I ragazzi corrono intorno
al fuoco
con le mani nelle mani,
smemorati,
come se avessero bevuto
del vino.
Per molto tempo si ricorderanno
con gioia
dei fuochi accesi in novembre
al limitare del campo.

Fires in November

They are burning weeds
in the fields
they set off a lively blaze
and a querulous smoke.
The white mist takes refuge
among the acacias
but the slow smoke coming up close
will not let it be.
The boys run round in a circle
about the fire
hand in hand,
absent-mindedly,
as if they were drunk
with wine.
For a long time they will remember
with delight
fires that men light in November
at the edges of the field.

La notte d'ottobre

Mi ha svegliato il tuo canto solitario,
triste amica dell'ottobre, innocente civetta.
Era la notte,
brulicante di sogni come api.

Ronzavano
agitando le chiome di fuoco
e le bionde barbe,
ma i loro occhi erano rossi e tristi.

Tu cantavi, malinconica
come una prigioniera orientale
sotto il cielo azzurro...
Io ascoltavo battere il mio cuore.

October Night

Your solitary song awakened me,
sad friend of October, innocent owl.
It was night,
swarming with dreams like bees.

They kept up their buzzing
agitating fiery tresses
and blond beards,
but their eyes were red and sad.

You sang, melancholy
as an oriental captive
under her azure sky...
I could hear the beating of my heart.

Pagina di diario

A Bologna, alla Fontanina,
un cameriere furbo e liso
senza parlare, con un sorriso
aprì per noi una porticina.

La stanza vuota e assolata dava
su un canale
per cui silenziosa, uguale,
una flotta d'anatre navigava.

Un vino d'oro splendeva nei bicchieri
che ci inebbriò;
l'amore, nei tuoi occhi neri,
fuoco in una radura, s'incendiò.

Page from a Diary

In Bologna at La Fontanina
the waiter was all blandness, guile,
who opened a little door for us
without a word and with a smile.

The empty room was full of sun:
beyond the window, a canal
where, moving smooth and silently,
a fleet of ducks came sailing down.

The wine was golden in the glass,
sparkling, inebriating us:
love within your dark eyes played
as running fire ignites a glade.

Amore a me...

Amore a me vicino
di tua crudeltà mi consola,
fuori è notte e cade
una dolce pioggia improvvisa.

La famigliare lampada rivela
le intime e care cose,
amore parla e parla di te
sommesso, come acqua fra erbe alte.

Love Close...

Love close to me
consoles me at your cruelty,
outside it is night-time and there falls
a soft rain unforeseen.

The household lamp reveals
the things one knows and cherishes,
love speaks and speaks of you
softly, like water between high grasses.

Ottobre

Nei mattini di ottobre
quando i sogni
di me fanciullo
cominciavano ad empirsi di brezza e di voci
(qualcuno aveva aperta una finestra
e se n'era andato lieve)
il treno che passava a quell'ora
non lontano, con la sua criniera di fumo
e i fischi, mi dava un dolce e muto terrore.
Io gli giacevo sotto, senza pensieri,
con il fragore nelle orecchie,
finché era passato tutto,
e la mamma correva verso di me
dall'orizzonte, sudata e fresca
in una vestaglia rosa.
Ero sveglio
e un'ape volava
per l'aria radiosa.
Avrei voluto chiamare e stavo zitto.

October

On mornings in October
when my childish dreams
were beginning to fill with breeze and voices
(someone had opened a window
and then stolen out),
the train which passed at that hour
not far away, with its mane of smoke
and its whistling, thrilled me with sweet mute terror.
I lay there beneath it, without a care,
with its roar in my ears
until all of it had passed,
and mother came running toward me
from the horizon, hot and youthful
in a pink dressing gown.
I was awake
and a bee was flying
through the radiant air.
I wanted to cry out and I kept silent.

Insonnia

Come cavallo
che meridiana ombra impaura
s'impunta il sonno,
finché l'alba sbianca l'oriente.
Allora, stanco, si rimette a trottare
per borgate che si svegliano,
davanti a osterie che riaprono
da cui escono voci
e un fresco odore di grappa.

Insomnia

Like a horse
that noonday shadows frighten
sleep stumbles,
until dawn whitens the east.
Then, tired, it begins to trot once more
through villages that are awakening,
past inns that are re-opening
from which issue voices
and a fresh whiff of grappa.

LETTERA DA CASA
LETTER FROM HOME
(1951)

Al fratello

Un giorno amaro l'infinita cerchia
dei colli
veste di luce declinante,
e già trabocca sulla pianura
un autunno di foglie.

Piu freddi ora dispiega i suoi vessilli
d'ombra il tramonto,
un chiaro lume nasce
dove tu dolce manchi
all'antica abitudine serale.

To My Brother

One grievous day
clothes the infinite circle of the hills
in a waning light,
and already there overflows across the plain
a whole autumn of leaves.

Colder the sunset now unfurls
its shadowy ensigns:
a bright lamp is lit
where you in your gentleness are missing
from the ancient ceremony of evening.

Per B...

I piccoli aeroplani di carta che tu
fai volano nel crepuscolo, si perdono
come farfalle notturne nell'aria
che s'oscura, non torneranno più.

Così i nostri giorni, ma un abisso
meno dolce li accoglie
di questa valle silente di foglie
morte e d'acque autunnali

dove posano le loro stanche ali
i tuoi fragili alianti.

For B...

The little paper planes you make
fly into twilight, disappear
like night-moths in the darkening air:
now they will never circle back.

Our days are like that, gathered in
by a less gradual abyss
than this valley, silent with
its dead leaves and autumnal rain

where, fragile, your imaginings
glide down to rest on tired wings.

At home

Il sole lentamente si sposta
sulla nostra vita, sulla paziente
storia dei giorni che un mite
calore accende, d'affetti e di memorie.

A quest'ora meridiana
lo spaniel invecchia sul mattone
tiepido, il tuo cappello di paglia
s'allontana nell'ombra della casa.

At Home

The sun moves slowly on
above our life, above the patient
story of the days that a mild warmth sets alight
with recollections and with love.

At this noonday hour
the spaniel ages on the warm
brick floor; your straw hat
disappears into the shadows of the house.

Gli anni

Le mattine dei nostri anni perduti,
i tavolini nell'ombra soleggiata dell'autunno,
i compagni che andavano e tornavano, i compagni
che non tornarono più, ho pensato ad essi lietamente.

Perché questo giorno di settembre splende
così incantevole nelle vetrine in ore
simili a quelle d'allora, quelle d'allora
scorrono ormai in un pacifico tempo,

la folla è uguale sui marciapiedi dorati,
solo il grigio e il lilla
si mutano in verde e rosso per la moda,
il passo è quello lento e gaio della provincia.

The Years

The mornings of our lost years,
the tables in the sunny autumn shade,
the friends who went and then returned, the friends
who will never return again, I thought of them with joy.

Because this September day is shining
so beguilingly into windows of shops in hours
like those of then; those of then
are gliding by at a peaceful tempo now,

the crowd is the same on golden pavements,
only the grey and lilac
are changed by fashion into green and red,
the pace is slow and easy, that of the provinces.

Aprile a B...

Oh, tu fra il grano in erba e la siepe
di biancospino fiorita
nell'ombrosa distanza che circonda
la tua infanzia romita,
questo giorno che un vento tenero annulla
un fresco sole inonda.
Ti muovi nel silenzio delicato
della natura che si fa gentile
e favoloso labirinto,
bambino perso in un'ora d'aprile.
Chi ti guarda non ode
le tue parole all'uomo che recide
i rami di gaggìa, ode
il pennato che stride nel vento più forte
e mischia quietamente vita e morte.

April for B...

Oh, you between the half-grown grain and hedge
of flowering hawthorn
in the shadowy distance which surrounds
your solitary childhood,
this day that a tender wind annuls
a cool sun inundates.
You move in the fragile silence
of nature now become
a benign and fabulous labyrinth,
child lost in an April hour.
Whoever watches you does not hear
your words to the man who lops away
the branches of the acacia, only hears
the swish of the billhook in the risen wind
tranquilly mingling life and death.

Lettera da casa

(inviando dei versi a Giorgio Bassani)

                          Qui è l'estate,
una sera dopo l'altra si aprono
le finestre per dare aria alle stanze,
allora riflettono gli specchi una campagna
che il cucù intermittente di lontano,
chi sa dove, immalinconisce.
Un alto carro di fieno si presenta
traballante, esce portandosi un ragazzo
perso nel raggio obliquo del tramonto
fra trofei verdi che già dolcemente
si piegano avvizziti. (Addio, addio,
uscito dallo specchio dove vai?
Oh, vicino, se si ode il tuo
parlottare indistinto, ma lontano
come se le nostre spoglie ormai
giacessero presso quelle che sono
chiuse nel muro sbiadito.)
Ora parla invisibile con uomini
che scaricano il carro nel fienile
e finito il lavoro lo isseranno
a quel rosone di mattoni tiepidi
che guarda verso la città distesa
in una vertigine di pianura aperta
nella sera.

Letter from Home
(sending verses to Giorgio Bassani)

            Here it is summer:
evening after evening they set wide
the windows to let air into the rooms,
then the mirrors reflect a countryside
that the intermittent cuckoo from afar,
from who knows where, tinges with melancholy.
A tall haywain sways into view,
vanishes bearing away a boy
lost in the slant ray of the sundown
among green trophies that already
are slowly withering. (Farewell, farewell,
gone from the mirror I can no longer tell
where you are bound for.
Oh, close by I should say
to judge from your half-heard chatter, and yet
distant as if our bones already lay
beside those that faded wall encloses.)
Now, unseen, he is talking with the men
who empty the cart into the haybarn
and, the job once done, will hoist him up
to that rose-window of brick still warm
which gazes towards the city spread
in a vertigo of open plain
in the evening.

A Giuseppe, in ottobre

Per quali strade di campagna vai
nel sole troppo caldo d'ottobre,
la mano chiusa in sé, la luce
a metà del tuo viso, a metà l'ombra?

È il quieto pomeriggio d'un bel giorno,
il bel giorno cammina coi tuoi passi
incerti fra le foglie che di ruggine
macchiano i rustici viali dell'Emilia.

Come il passero arrossa le sue penne
e ci dice che è il mattino ancora
tu camminando assorto fai che venga
sera e accogli nella pupilla severa

di bambino i colori del tramonto.
Così per me s'apre e si chiude un giorno
d'autunno, entro vi si muove gente
di queste parti, e si ferma e discorre,

o tira via, saluta, altra porta
secchi d'acqua lontana. Presto
sarà l'inverno, lasciate che fermi
la stagione che indugia su una trama paziente.

To Giuseppe, in October

Along what country by-roads do you go
in the too hot October sun,
with hands tight-clenched, the light upon
half your face, the other half shadow?

The quiet afternoon of a fine day:
the fine day travels with your uncertain
steps among the leaves that stain
rust-red Emilia's rural pathways.

As redness dawns on the sparrow's feathers
that tells us it is still early morning,
so your thoughtful pacing signals evening
and your grave child's pupil gathers

into itself the colours of sundown.
And so one autumn day opens and closes for me,
during which the people of the vicinity
pass, pause to talk, press on

with a murmured greeting, some
trundle their buckets of water from far away:
winter will soon be here, but let it stay
this season lingering over its patient loom.

LA CAPANNA INDIANA

THE INDIAN WIGWAM

(1955)

La capanna indiana: I

Dietro la casa s'alza nella nebbia
di novembre il suo culmine indeciso:
una semplice costruzione rurale
ai limiti dei campi, una graziosa
parvenza sulla bruma che dirada,
si direbbe una capanna indiana.
Qui dove gli attrezzi da lavoro
giacciono rovesciati poi che il sole
estremo di stagione ha chiuso il ciclo
delle semine, con accorta mano
i pali furono incrociati l'uno
contro l'altro così da ricavarne
un padiglione quieto nell'autunno.
Sulla terra indurita che conduce
al solitario ritrovo saltella
l'uccellino che chiamano del freddo
e non s'accorge delle altre presenze
sul sentiero, diretto forse a qualche
ultima bacca rosseggiante al suo
occhio acuto e tranquillo, di lontano.
Ma noi, noi quale promessa porta
nell'aria fredda del mattino a tanto
abbandono? Quale dolce cibo
per le nostre bocche di fanciulli
al di là del silenzio familiare,
oltre l'ultima paglia marcia, dove
il sentiero finisce, dove il sentiero muore?
Ora il giorno è sereno su tutta
la pianura sin dove la città
appare, chiuso sogno a noi, segreto,
di grige e rosse dimore silenti
frammezzo i tronchi nudi delle piante.
Oh, sarà un tempo così calmo,
segnato appena dal gentile invito
del venditore ambulante nel sole
di mezzogiorno, dal rumore netto
d'un sasso contro l'azzurra grondaia.
Allora nel silenzio udremo il grido
dei nostri cari, sempre più vicino

The Indian Wigwam: I

Behind the house there rises through the fog
of November its uncertain peak:
a simple, rural structure
at the edge of the fields, a graceful
apparition in the thinning mist –
an Indian wigwam, one might have said.
Here, where the implements of labour
lie scattered all around
since the last warmth of the season put an end
to the cycle of sowing, with a shrewd hand
the stakes were leaned up crossways
one against another so as to make of them
a quiet pavilion in the autumn.
On the hardened ground which leads
to this solitary haunt the tiny bird
they say means cold is coming
hops now and gives no heed to other presences
along the path, on the move perhaps
towards some one remaining berry
brightly reddening in its sharp and steady eye
from afar. But as for us, what promise
in the chilly air of morning
carries us to such abandonment?
What sweet food for our childish mouths,
beyond the silent house,
past the last rotting straw
where the pathway ends, dies out?
Now the day is cloudless
over all the plain right on up to where
the town appears, to us a dream undreamt,
secret, its houses red and grey, silent
among the bare trunks of the trees.
Oh, this day will be so calm
its passing scarcely hinted by the courteous call
of the pedlar in the noonday sun,
by the clean sound of the pebble flung in play
against the blue guttering.
Then in the silence we shall hear the cry
of our parents, ever nearer

e ansioso, poi fioco, perduto
nella nebbia che rapida s'addensa
di questi giorni appena il sole volge
oltre il meriggio e pare che la notte
discenda ormai, senza speranza.

L'erba che tocca fredda i nostri corpi
distesi e accovacciati dentro l'ombra,
i nostri visi nascosti, i ginocchi dolenti,
è già una dura erba d'inverno, morta.
Eppure è il tempo più dolce dell'anno
quando la siepe brulla che recinge
del suo braccio il deserto dominio
si fa intima stanza allo smarrito
passero già colore della terra.
Qui siamo giunti dove volevamo,
nel mattino nebbioso camminare
non stanca, e quando passa una carretta
con rumore di latte sballottato
nello zinco che luce ad una spera
fuggitiva di sole l'uomo dorme,
anche il cavallo dorme e s'allontana
incerto con il suo trotto paziente.

La casa si vedeva appena, presa
nel sonno triste di un'alba qualunque
di novembre, a una svolta dove al tempo
di Pasqua s'odono le campane sciolte
vibrare nella terra che si bacia.
Era l'ora che dietro alle persiane
la famiglia si desta amaramente,
l'ultima mosca ronza moribonda
nella chiusa cucina ove la brace
dei primi fuochi autunnali dura
sino alla prima donna freddolosa,
giovane strega, montanara falsa.
Al suo soffio, al suo abile maneggio
di stecchi già s'illumina la stanza
che la finestra aperta ora riempie
di nebbia a folate intermittenti.
Ma il tempo passa ed altre finestre
si disserrano al giorno senza voglia,

and more anxious, then feeble, lost
in the sudden, thickening fog
of these days when sunlight scarcely lasts
beyond noon and when it seems that night
comes down already, without hope.

The grass that touches our bodies coldly
where we lie crouching in the darkness,
with muffled faces, aching knees,
is already the hard, dead grass of winter.
And yet it is the sweetest time of all the year
when the bare hedge that encloses
with its arm the empty domain
makes of itself an intimate room
for the stray sparrow, the colour of earth already.
We have arrived here where we wished –
walking in the foggy morning
is not tiring, and when a cart goes by
with the sound of slapping milk inside the churn
that shines out in a fleeting ray
the man is asleep,
the horse slumbers too as it moves
uncertainly away with patient trot.

The house could scarcely be seen,
caught in the sad sleep of a common dawn
in November, at a turn of the road,
where you can hear round Eastertime
the scattered chime of bells vibrate
in the ground we children kiss.
It was the hour when behind the shutters
the family comes painfully awake;
a last fly buzzes half-dead
in the close kitchen where the embers
of the first autumnal fires await
the first servant chilled with cold,
young witch, deceitful woman of the mountains.
At her breath, at her careful handling
of the sticks the room is lit up already
whose open window now admits
the fog in fitful gusts. But time is passing
and other shutters will be unlocked

toccano lente l'edera stracciata
e l'intonaco fragile. Ci siamo
seduti sulla terra arata, quieti,
guardandoci attorno, sgretolando
una zolla appena umida del fiato
di bruma che si va alzando adagio
sul passo di due ragazzi soli
prima, poi sempre meno distanti,
finché si vedono avanzare insieme
e scomparire parlottando, amici
di tanti giorni lunghi in un tempo
che non finisce mai.

E come dolcemente il giorno cresce
sulla pianura seminata ormai
pronta al riposo dell'inverno, eppure
oggi perduta dietro il sole ultimo
che matura sui tralci rari grani
abbandonati anche dagli storni.
Al suo calore il muro della casa
intiepidisce, un calcinaccio cade
con un tonfo attutito dai rametti
del rosmarino arido, una donna
canta felice da una stanza aperta
che di qua non si vede, solitaria
voce del tempo bello e dell'oblio.
Nessuno si ricorda, tanto cara
è l'ora trascorrente sulla terra
che un uccello lontano e silenzioso
segna della sua ombra fuggitiva,
nessuno si ricorda più di noi.

to let in the listless day
and graze the ragged ivy
and the fragile plaster. We are sitting
on the ploughed earth, silent,
gazing round us, crumbling
a clod that's barely dampened by the breath
of fog now rising slowly
before the feet of two boys separate
at first, then gradually less distant,
until you see them both approach together
and chatting disappear, friends
of so many endless days, in a time
that will never be over.

And how gently the day grows
across the plain now planted,
ready for the repose of winter, yet
lost today behind the last sun
which is ripening sparse grapes on the vine-branch
abandoned even by the starlings.
In its heat the wall of the house
is growing warm, the plaster falls
with a sound deadened by the stalks
of dried-up rosemary; a woman
is singing gaily at an open window
unseen from here, the solitary voice
of happiness and oblivion.
No one remembers, so precious
is the hour elapsing now on earth
which a distant silent bird
marks with its fugitive shadow,
no one remembers us any more.

Da La capanna indiana II

Come agosto finisce la mattina
dopo una notte di pioggia si sente
(il cielo è più profondo) che l'autunno
sta per venire, ci si guarda intorno
e non si sa che fare, tutto
è fresco, rinnovato da uno smalto
malinconico di perplessità.
Allora si gironzola, si sta zitti,
sappiamo che c'è tempo, ma che pure
l'anno dovrà morire, ed il bel cielo,
il verde verniciato delle piante,
il rosso delle ruote ad asciugare,
l'incudine che suona di lontano,
lento cuore del giorno, tutto parla
d'una partenza prossima, un addio.

La memoria è una strada che si perde
e si ritrova dopo un'ansia breve,
tranquilla, già nel sole di settembre
scottante sulla schiena è un'altra estate
che le vespe ronzando sulle ceste
dell'uva bianca indorano e si mischia
al loro volo il rumore nascosto
e perenne del grano che ventila
un vecchio attento e polveroso.
Finché c'è lui in giro il tempo è buono
da noi […]

From **The Indian Wigwam** II

As August ends, on a morning
after a night of rain you feel
(the sky is deeper now) that autumn
is about to come, you gaze and gaze
uncertain what to do; all
is fresh, renewed
by a mournful sheen of perplexity.
You wander out, incapable of speech,
knowing that there is time and yet
that the year must die, and the clear sky,
the painted green of plants,
the red of wheels drying in the sun,
the anvil ringing in the distance,
slow heartbeat of the day, all speaks
of a parting now at hand, of last words.

Memory is a path one loses
and after sudden uncertainty finds again
still serene; already in the September sun
another summer scorches at your back
to which the wasps add their flecks of gold
buzzing above baskets of white grapes,
and there mingles with their wings
the hidden and perennial sound of grain
an old, intent, dust-whitened man
is winnowing. The weather will stay fine
so long as he is active in the scene. [...]

IN UN TEMPO INCERTO
IN AN UNCERTAIN TIME

(1955)

Pensieri di casa

Non posso più scrivere né vivere
se quest'anno la neve che si scioglie
non mi avrà testimone impaziente
di sentire nell'aria prime viole.

Come se fossi morto mi ricordo
la nostra primavera, la sua luce
esultante che dura tutto un giorno,
la meraviglia di un giorno che passa.

Forse a noi ultimi figli dell'età
impressionista non è dato altro
che copiare dal vero, mentre sgoccia
la neve su dei passeri aggruppati.

[Roma 1952]

Home Thoughts

I can no longer write nor even live
if the melting of the snow this year
will not have me as a witness
impatient to smell the first violets in the air.

As if I were one of the dead, I can recall
our own spring, its exultant light
that lasts all through the day,
the marvel of a day that passes.

Perhaps nothing else is left for us to do,
late children of the impressionist era,
except to copy from the real while snow
drips down onto a gathering of sparrows.

[Rome 1952]

A sua madre, che aveva nome Maria

Sei tu, invocata ogni sera, dipinta sulle nuvole
che arrossano la nostra pianura e chi si muove in essa,
bambini freschi come foglie e donne umide in viaggio
verso la città nella luce d'un acquazzone che smette,
sei tu, madre giovane eternamente in virtù della morte
che t'ha colta, rosa sul punto dolce di sfioritura,
tu, l'origine di ogni nevrosi e ansia che mi tortura,
e di questo ti ringrazio per l'età passata presente e futura.

To His Mother Whose Name Was Maria

It is you, invoked every evening, depicted on the clouds
that redden our open plain and those who move in it,
with children as fresh as leaves and wet women travelling
towards the city in the light of a shower just ending,
it is you, mother forever young in virtue of the death
that plucked you, rose at that point just before the petals fall,
you who are the origin of every neurosis and anxiety that is my torture,
and for this I thank you for time past present and future.

Frammento
(escluso dalla «Capanna indiana»)

Quei nuvolosi, inerti giorni quando
opaco argento è il cielo, dove volgere
svogliati, chiusi nella nostra pena?
C'è un portico di pochi attrezzi e fieno
rimasto, un luogo ove nessuno viene
a quest'ora incerta del giorno, marzo
è un mese di transito, sediamo
chini a un gioco di polvere e di stecchi,
qualche parola cade, qualche goccia
rada di pioggia, e smette nel silenzio
di quest'ultimo luogo della terra
dove il corpo irrequieto trovi posa.
In un umile, abbandonato portico,
nel grigio corso di un mattino abbiamo
sentito fra le mani senza scopo
fluire tempo e polvere di giochi.
Ma lasciate che io lodi anche il pallore
dell'aria di quel vuoto giorno perso
se oggi ad esso sorride amaramente
la cara compagnia e ansiosa guarda.

Fragment
(left out of 'The Indian Wigwam')

Those days of stagnancy and cloudy threat
when the sky is silver yet quite lustreless,
where shall we turn in our indifference?
This open shed remains, it holds a few
scattered implements, beside some hay,
empty, at this uncertain hour of day.
March is a busy month, so let us sit
crouched above our games with sticks and dust;
a few words fall, a drop or two of rain,
then leave off in the silence of this last
place in all the world where one might say
the body's restlessness is safely past.
Within a humble and abandoned yard
in the grey fading of one morning we
felt through our hands bereft of any aim
time trickle and the dry dust of our game.
Yet let me even praise the pallor then,
the atmosphere of an empty day that's done,
if, wistful, they can spare a smile for it,
my dear companions, threatened once again.

Il frate

Viene un frate alla mia casa porta
la prima polvere attaccata ai sandali

viene a piedi lo segue un asinello
viene a cercare legna grano e melica

nei prati dolcemente asciuga l'ultimo
umido della neve che s'è sciolta

viene il frate più presso alla mia porta
uomo e animale aspettano nel sole

fiumi azzurri lambiscono la terra
bambini escono dall'ombra rospi e viole

pace feriale è questa che un'incudine
percossa chi sa dove segna e spande

a metà è la mia vita a metà il giorno
a metà ormai la mia solitudine.

The Friar

A friar comes up to my house he brings
the first dust clinging to his sandals

he comes on foot an ass following on behind
wood wheat and millet are what he has in mind

in the meadows little by little the last
dampness is drying out from the snow now past

the friar comes up closer to my door
man and beast both wait in the sun out there

blue rivers are lapping the ground where they flow
children toads and violets emerge from shadow

this is the peace of an ordinary day that an anvil
struck somewhere marks and expands in a swell of sound

my life is half done midway the day
and now my solitude cut in half as well.

Le formiche

Le formiche sul tronco adulto della gaggìa
profittano del sole che scalda i giorni d'ottobre,
minuto per minuto, su e giù per la scorza ruvida.

In faccende le formiche per l'inverno che viene,
se sposto l'occhio alla luce della strada maestra
vedo in faccende passare uomini e donne su e giù.

O unanime lena di esseri viventi con me
in questa pianura che si prepara coraggiosa alla neve
aiutami ad affrontare lo smorzarsi del giorno,

l'accendersi della notte sulle nostre case disuguali.

The Ants

The ants on the full-grown trunk of the acacia
profit from the sun that warms October days,
minute by minute, up and down on the rough bark of the tree.

The ants are toiling against the coming winter:
if I shift my glance to the light of the highway here
it is men and women I see toiling up and down.

O single spirit of beings who live beside me
on this open plain bravely preparing to face the snow
help me confront the extinction of the daylight,

over our unequal houses the kindling night.

I bambini, dopo scuola vengono mandati per viole

Ci vogliono molte viole
raccolte con la pazienza
che il bambino nel fondo
dell'essere spontaneamente
quando è il suo tempo coglie
segreta come la viola
che stava sotto le foglie.

Ci vogliono molte viole
per farne un mazzetto odoroso
e non ha la campagna
di questa stagione altri fiori
da portare a quei morti
che nel bambino chinato
rinascono, nei suoi gesti assorti.

Children, Sent Out after School for Violets

What we want are lots of violets
gathered with the patience
that spontaneously takes possession of a child
deep inside its being
when the time comes round –
patience as secret as the violet
as it waited beneath the leaves close to the ground.

What we want are lots of violets
to make of them an odorous nosegay
and they are the only flower
the country has to offer at this season
to carry to those dead
who in the bending child are born again
where he moves about lost in concentration.

VIAGGIO D'INVERNO
WINTER JOURNEY
(1971)

I papaveri

Questo è un anno di papaveri, la nostra
terra ne traboccava poi che vi tornai
fra maggio e giugno, e m'inebriai
d'un vino così dolce così fosco.

Dal gelso nuvoloso al grano all'erba
maturità era tutto, in un calore
conveniente, in un lento sopore
diffuso dentro l'universo verde.

A metà della vita ora vedevo
figli cresciuti allontanarsi soli
e perdersi oltre il carcere di voli
che la rondine stringe nello spento

bagliore d'una sera di tempesta,
e umanamente il dolore cedeva
alla luce che in casa s'accendeva
d'un'altra cena in un'aria più fresca

per grandine sfogatasi lontano.

Poppies

This is a year of poppies. Our land
was overflowing with them when I returned
between May and June, and they intoxicated me
with such a sweet and such a dusky wine.

From the cloudy mulberry to the grain and grass
ripeness was all, in a heat
not too hot, in a drowsiness
diffused across this universe of green.

Half-way through my life, I'd seen
grown sons go off into their own
world, lost to sight beyond the cage in flights
which the swallows weave across the spent

glare of a stormy evening
and as is natural, my sorrow subsided
in the light of the house re-kindled
for another meal in an atmosphere freshened now

by a scattering of hailstones in the distance.

Le farfalle

Perché le farfalle vanno sempre a due a due
e se una si perde entro il cespo violetto
delle settembrine l'altra non la lascia ma sta
sopra e vola confusa che pare si sbatta
contro i muri di un carcere mentre non è che questo
oro del giorno già in via d'offuscarsi
alle cinque del pomeriggio avvicinandosi ottobre?

– Forse credevi d'averla perduta ma eccola ancora
sospesa nell'aria riprendere l'irragionevole moto
verso le plaghe che l'ombra più presto fa sue
dei campi vendemmiati e arati della domenica:
tu non hai che a seguirla incontro alla notte
come l'attendesti nel lume inquieto del sole
finché fu sazia del succo di quei fiori d'autunno.

Butterflies

Why is it butterflies always go two by two
and if one disappears into a clump
of September violets the other does not leave it
but hovers on there confused as if
beating against the walls of a prison which is only
the gold of day already tarnishing
at five in the afternoon as October closes in?

Perhaps you thought you had lost her but there she is
once more suspended in air starting all over again
that absurd movement of hers towards regions that the dark
claims more swiftly from the harvested ploughed Sunday vineyards:
you have only to follow her towards the night
as you awaited her in the restless sunlight
till she was sated with the nectar of autumn flowers.

Gli imbianchini sono pittori

(a Roberto Longhi)

Arrivò prima il figlio, in quell'ora
lucente dopo il pasto il sole e il vino,
eppure silenziosa, tanto che
si sentiva il pennello sul muro
distendere il celeste. Non guardava
fuori, la sua giovinezza
e salute gli bastava, attento
alla precisione dei bordi turchini
entro cui asciugando già l'azzurro
scoloriva com'era giusto. Allora
venne il padre che recava uno stampo,
il verde il rosso e il rosa,
e la stanchezza degli anni e il pallore.
Doveva su quel cielo preparato
con cura far fiorire le rose,
ma il verde stemperato per le foglie
non gli andava, non era un verde quale
ai suoi occhi deboli brillava all'esterno
con disperata intensità appressandosi
la sera che si porta via i colori.
Le corolle vermiglie ombrate in rosa
fiorirono più tardi la stanza,
una qua una là, accordate
alle ultime dell'orto, e il buio,
fuori e dentro, compì un giorno
non inutile che lascia a chi verrà,
e dormirà e si sveglierà fra questi
muri, la gioia delle rose e del cielo.

Decorators are Artists
(to Roberto Longhi)

The son was the first to arrive, at that shining hour
after the midday meal, the sun and wine,
shining and yet silent, so much so
that you could hear the brush against the wall
spreading its blue. He did not look
outside, his youthfulness
and good health sufficed him, his mind
intent on the precision of the dark-blue borders
within which the lighter blue already drying
was fading as it should. Then
came the father bringing a stencil for the repeats,
along with the green, the red and pink
and the weariness of his years and the pallor.
What he had to do on that prepared sky
was carefully to make the roses bloom,
but the feeble green did not suit him
for the leaves, it was nothing like the green
which his weak eyes saw glow outdoors
with desperate intensity when the evening
that takes away the colours was drawing near.
The crimson corollas, shaded into pink,
later on lit up the room with blossom,
one here, one there, matching
the latest in the garden, and the dark,
outside and within completed a day
not wasted, leaving for whoever comes,
and sleeps and wakes between these walls,
the delight of the roses and the sky.

La teleferica

(a B, con una otto millimetri)

L'estate impolvera le siepi
anche oltre i mille metri,
impolvera le more ostinate
in un'adolescenza agra.

Ma la tua adolescenza s'addolcisce, matura
nella pazienza artigiana e sottile
di questa ripresa dal basso
e da dietro la siepe stracciata,
così da tramare di spini foglie e bacche
il racconto nel suo tempo reale
scandito dai passi silenziosi
e furtivi dei bambini Giuseppe Marta
Galeazzina «fuggiti di casa»
quando tutti dormono a Casarola
perché è luglio e il fuoco meridiano
piega anche la gente selvatica
dell'Appennino, anche le donne
indomabili nell'avarizia e nella sporcizia.
boccheggianti su pagliericci miseri
in triste pace.

Soltanto voi, gentili villeggianti,
vivete quest'ora, ne rubate
l'acuta fiamma sì che i vostri occhi
rideranno, nel primo piano, per sempre
al sole delle tre.

Affrettatevi, la teleferica è lontana
e Bernardo, che ha le gambe lunghe
dei quattordici anni, la smania dello story-teller,
insiste sul tempo reale, vuole
che vi perdiate fra castagni e felci
a cercare, con la luce che si fa
più e più debole – affrettatevi,
la sera è paurosa sui monti –
i fili metallici che tagliano le mani
e portano via il legname

The Cableway

(to B, with an eight millimetre cine camera)

Summer covers the hedges with dust
even at over a thousand metres,
it covers with dust the persistent blackberries
in their sour adolescence.

But your adolescence sweetens, matures
in the subtle craftsman's patience
with which you shoot from below
and from behind the ragged hedge, so weaving
its real time of berries, thorns and leaves
into the story pulsating in the furtive steps
of the children Giuseppe, Marta
Galeazzina 'the runaways',
while all sleep at Casarola
because it is July and the fire of noon
weighs even on the wild folk
of the Apennines, even the women
indomitable in their avarice and filth,
breathless on wretched mattresses
in sorry peace.

Only you, gentle vacationers,
are living this hour, stealing
the intense flame of it, so that your eyes
will smile, in close-up, for ever
in the three o'clock sun.

Hurry, the cableway is far off
and Bernardo, who has the long legs
of a fourteen-year-old, the obsession of the storyteller
insists on real time, wants you
to lose yourselves among the chestnuts and the bracken
seeking under a light that grows
fainter and fainter – hurry,
night is frightening on the hills –
the metal wires that cut hands
and carry away the timber

per il tannino, o lo portavano, la fabbrica
va in pezzi, e le funi intrecciate
ci voleva Giuseppe a scoprirle, perse
nella vertigine dei rami più alti,
ruggine e clorofilla, avventura e terrore
di un bambino che gioca: questo
l'antefatto del racconto, ora egli
conduce le cugine più grandi
all'altalena sospirata
e non la troverà più,
il suo cuore ne sentirà dolore,
quale soltanto, passati anni e anni infiniti,
l'uomo prova nel primo orgasmo dell'infarto.

L'ultima inquadratura è dall'alto
di un ramo di cerro, l'occhio della macchina
ricerca inquieto i tuoi occhi inquieti,
guida sconfitta,
mentre già le bambine si distraggono,
la più grande delle sorelle intreccia
un cappello di foglie sui capelli
della più piccola, l'operatore-poeta
se ne innamora anche lui, pensa all'effetto
che ne ricaverà quando avvizzite
le foglie finiranno sulla polvere
rosata del crepuscolo freddo
sulla via del ritorno, scordati
il dolore precoce, la pupilla delusa,
il tema umano della novelletta.
Lasciate che l'arte si prenda
queste rivincite improvvise ma giuste
sulla vita, che un ragazzo ne profitti
e abbia coscienza in quei cari anni
della vocazione e dell'apprendistato.

for making tannin, carried, rather:
the factory is falling to ruin, and it took
Giuseppe to find the tangled cables, lost
in the vertigo of the highest boughs,
rust and chlorophil, adventure and terror
of a child at play: all this
just the prelude to the story, now he
leads the girls, his older cousins
up to the dreamed-of swing
and will not find it any more;
his heart will feel the pain of it
such as only the man, years and infinite years later,
experiences in the first great agitation
of the heart's obstructed vein.

The last take is from above
high on an oak branch, the camera's eye
anxiously seeks out your troubled eyes,
guide discomfitted,
while already the girls are amusing themselves;
the elder sister weaves
over the hair of the younger
a hat of leaves, the poet–cameraman
is captivated too, he is considering the effect
that he will get from it once those leaves
withered, finish up in the rosy dust
of a cold twilight, forgotten
on the way back, forgotten too
the premature pain, the eye's disappointed pupil
the human theme of the little story.
Do not begrudge art taking for itself
these unforeseen but just revenges
on life, so that a boy profit from them,
know them for what they are in each precious year
of a vocation and apprenticeship.

Verso Casarola

Lasciate che m'incammini per la strada in salita
e al primo batticuore mi volga,
già da stanchezza e gioia esaltato ed oppresso,
a guardare le valli azzurre per la lontananza,
azzurre le valli e gli anni
che spazio e tempo distanziano.
Così a una curva, vicina
tanto che la frescura dei fitti noccioli e d'un'acqua
pullulante perenne nel cavo gomito d'ombra
giunge sin qui dove sole e aria baciano la fronte le mani
di chi ha saputo vincere la tentazione al riposo,
io veda la compagnia sbucare e meravigliarsi di tutto
con l'inquieta speranza dei migratori e dei profughi
scoccando nel cielo il mezzogiorno montano
del 9 settembre '43. Oh, campane
di Montebello Belasola Villula Agna ignare,
stordite noi che camminiamo in fuga
mentre immobili guardano da destra e da sinistra
più in alto più in basso nel faticato appennino
dell'aratura quelli cui toccherà pagare
anche per noi insolventi,
ma ora pacificamente lasciano splendere il vomere
a solco incompiuto, asciugare il sudore, arrestarsi
il tempo per speculare sul fatto
che un padre e una madre giovani un bambino e una serva
s'arrampicano svelti, villeggianti fuori stagione
(o gentile inganno ottico del caldo mezzodì),
verso Casarola ricca d'asini di castagni e di sassi.

Potessero ascoltare, questi che non sanno ancora nulla,
noi che parliamo, rimasti un po' indietro,
perdutisi la ragazza e il bambino più sù in un trionfo
inviolato di more ritardatarie e dolcissime,
potessi io, separato da quel giovane
intrepido consiglio di famiglia in cammino,
tenuto dopo aver deciso già tutto, tutto gettato nel piatto
della bilancia con santo senso del giusto,
oggi che nell'orecchio invecchiato e smagrito mi romba
il vuoto di questi anni buttati via. Perché,

Towards Casarola

Let me set out along the uphill way
and, at the first quickening heartbeat, turn,
uplifted and oppressed by my fatigue and joy,
to see the valleys' blueness league on league
(how blue the blueness that appears
down valleys distanced by both space and years).
Thus, at a curve,
so near that the coolness of thick hazels and of water
springing perennial in the depths of shade
reaches to here where sun and air caress the brow and hands
of one who resists the temptation of repose,
may I see our little band emerge, marvelling at all
with the unquiet hope of migrant and of fugitive,
the mountain midday chiming in the sky
of the 9th of September '43. Oh, bells
of Montebello, Belasola, Villula, Agna
unsuspecting, stun us as we pass in flight
while watching us from left and right
above, below, amid the ploughland
of the mountain inclines, stand unmoving
they who for our insolvency must also pay
but, now, peaceably let the blade shine out
in the uncompleted furrow, let the sweat dry
and time stand still, to speculate
that a father and a mother (both are young), their child and maid
come swiftly climbing, on unseasonable holiday
(how merciful the eyes' deceit at burning noon),
toward Casarola rich in asses, chestnuts, stone.

Would they could hear our words! – they to whom
the tale is still untold, as we linger in the rear,
the child and girl gone on ahead and lost among the untouched
full-flavoured glory of late-ripening blackberries;
would I could, too – separated from that youthful, bold
family council in flight that we had only begun to hold
long after all had been decided, all cast
in the balance with a sacred sense of right –
today, when in my aged, diminished ear
there roars the vacancy of year on year

chi meglio di un uomo e di una donna in età
di amarsi e amare il frutto dell'amore,
avrebbe potuto scegliere, maturando quel caldo
e troppo calmo giorno di settembre, la strada
per la salvezza dell'anima e del corpo congiunti
strettamente come sposa e sposo nell'abbraccio?
Scende, o sale, verso casa dai campi
gente di Montebello prima, poi di Belasola, assorta
in un lento pensiero, e già la compagnia forestiera
s'è ricomposta, appare impicciolita più in alto
finché l'inghiotte la bocca fresca d'un bosco
di cerri: là
c'è una fontana fresca nel ricordo
di chi guida e ha deciso
una sosta nell'ombra sino a quando i rondoni
irromperanno nel cielo che fu delle allodole. Allora
sarà tempo di caricare il figlio in cima alle spalle,
che all'uscita del folto veda con meraviglia
mischiarsi fumo e stelle su Casarola raggiunta.

now thrown away. Who better than a woman and a man
in the full freshness of their love, and loving the fruit
that came of it, to have dared (in the maturing
of that hot, too calm September day) to choose a way
for the salvation both of spirit and of flesh
clasped together as man and wife in close embrace?
Uphill or down, people from Montebello first,
and then from Belasola, trace back from the fields
their homeward track, absorbed in unhurried thought,
and now already the band of strangers has reunited,
showing smaller on their height
till the cool mouth of an oakwood
has swallowed them from sight: a spring runs fresh there
in the recollection of the one who leads the way
and has decreed a halt beneath the shade till the swifts
erupt into a sky that skylarks filled. Then
will be the time to hoist their son onto his shoulders,
so that emerging from the covert he can eye with awe
the mingling of smoke and stars above Casarola gained.

Aspettando la pioggia

Che ne sarà di noi se nuvole
non se ne presenteranno più
in questa terra amata proprio
per la sua verde umidità,

se le scorte finiranno prima
dell'inverno per noi e per
gli animali e il tempo bello
umetterà ogni mattina gli orli

delle finestre come un veleno
e la luna ogni notte entrerà
nelle nostre stanze impedendoci
di dormire, se non sapremo più

che fiori portare a coloro
che ci aspettano per chiederci
come mai ancora non li ha
svegliati verso l'alba il rumore

della pioggia sui coppi bruniti
così che possa riprendere
il discorso interrotto un altro
autunno quando l'amore

durava sino alla consumazione del dolore?

Waiting for Rain

What will become of us if clouds
never again appear
in this land we love precisely
because of its green humidity,

if the provisions for us and the animals
are to be exhausted before the winter
and the fine weather only moistens
each morning the corners

of the windows like a poison
and the moon each night
enters our rooms refusing
to let us sleep, if we no longer know

what flowers to take to those
who are waiting for us and want to ask
whyever it is that they have still
not been wakened at dawn by the sound

of rain on the burnished tiles
so that we may take up once again
the interrupted theme
of another autumn when love lasted

even until the consummation of sorrow?

Presso la Maestà B, un giorno d'agosto

Oggi non prenderò la strada che porta a Riana,
tagliata di recente nel fianco tenero del monte
sanguinante di faggi, lagrimoso d'acque bambine,
oggi non prenderò la strada nuova, non ancora
finita, strappata per il bene pubblico al chiuso
interesse dei miseri padroni di terre e boschi,
volta al futuro, azzurra di pozzanghere,

perché mi chiama, essendo domenica, l'irta
mulattiera in rovina verso Montebello arroccata
sul Bratica senza fiducia, fornitrice
ormai inutile di parenti e di preti,
selvosa di castagni un tempo primari
dispensatori d'alimenti alla gente di qui,
oggi, ultima domenica d'agosto, fitti
di frutti che nessuno spia ansioso
della loro gonfiezza anche se un cielo
vulnerato qua e là da lame preautunnali
nell'ardore del giorno ci parla
dell'approssimarsi di una stagione non mite.

Mentre cammino, sicuro di non trovare
nessuno per la via abbandonata,
fra gazze bianche e nere sull'oro
fosco di letamai decrepiti e bisce
spinte dalla siccità, presto perdute all'occhio
non alla mente che il peccato tortura,
odo gli ultimi botti della messa e m'affretto
pauroso che non m'inseguano e trattengano
dall'imboccare il sentiero in salita,
appena visibile sotto le foglie i sassi
che ne ingombrano il tremulo tracciato, da tanti
e tanti anni sconsacrato e deluso.

Ora, giunto a mezza costa, sento
il piede e il cuore sospendersi incerti
mentre dall'alto scivola, scoccando l'ora di fuoco,
una frana d'azzurro che allontana l'autunno,
e di fianco, sul lato sinistro, geme

Near Shrine B on an August Day

Today I shall not take the Riana road
cut lately into the tender mountain flank
bleeding with beeches, weeping with tiny streams;
today I shall not take the new, the still unfinished road
torn for the public good
from the tight-fistedness of owners of land and woodland,
facing the future, blue with its pools of rain;

for it is Sunday and the stone-strewn
ruinous mule-track calls me towards Montebello
perched warily above the Bratica,
useless breeder now of kin and clergy,
wooded round with chestnut trees,
chief providers once of food to these
hill-folk here; now – Sunday at August's end –
dense with fruits that no one eyes
anxious for their fulness, even though the skies
gashed here and there by pre-autumnal blades
tell us, in the heat of the day,
of an approaching season no longer mild.

As I press on, sure of finding
no one along the abandoned way,
among magpies white and black against the dusky gold
of decrepit dungheaps, snakes
driven by drought, soon lost to the eye
but not to the mind tortured by sin,
I hear the last bell-strokes of mass and hurry on
afraid I shall be followed and held back
from entering the track that leads uphill,
hardly visible beneath the leaves, the stones,
which encumber its tremulous line, for years
on years despised and deconsecrated.

Now, having climbed halfway, I feel
the hesitation of both foot and heart
when, from above, as the hour of fire strikes,
plunges an avalanche of blue that keeps back autumn;
and on the other side, sinister in both senses,

nell'ombra delle piante la camola che vive
sulla morte del legno. Non esito più, volgo
i miei passi fuori
dello spiazzo che mi tenne nel dubbio
e mi è già dietro le spalle, empio
di sole, io perdutamente
preso dal folto biondo bruno, dal soffoco
dolciastro, organico del bosco
in cui m'aspetta, colpa
e pentimento, unico bene,
la madre giovinetta.
Era te che cercavo, e non credevo
di trovarti così
a portata di tutti coloro, passeggeri
o legnaiuoli affaticati in transito,
che vogliano un riparo o un conforto.
Infatti la maestà cui sono giunto dinanzi
con tanta pena da monte,
s'offre allo sguardo subito, diroccata (eppure la sola
con la sua capannuccia sporgente capace
di tenere sotto nell'inclemenza del tempo),
a chi sale da valle e non può non vederne la mole
insolita fra gli altri tabernacoli
che s'incontrano, umili, qua e là
segnati di omaggi e di sfregi infantili.

Ma devo rallegrarmi, non cadere
in una vaneggiante tristezza, scoperto
che la cappella chiusa e quasi irraggiungibile
a me venuto per il cammino dei morti,
guidato dalla memoria, privilegio amaro
dei più gelosi spenditori di gioie,
assolva umana e così agevole ai suoi
compiti protettivi del corpo e dell'anima
se uno non la cerchi ma la trovi per strada,
aperta a tutti, ormai senza più nome.

Nessuno certo ha portato sassi
e calcina,
o la fina sabbia dalle chiare rive
del Bratica che scorre nella lunga
fonda ferita della terra, nessuno

in the shade of vegetation gnaws the beetle which survives
on the death of timber. I hesitate no longer, turn
my steps beyond
the clearing that held me there in doubt
and is already behind me, profane
with sun – I, surrendered unresisting now
to the tawny dark, the organic
sickly sweet oppression of the wood
where there awaits me, guilt
and penitence, sole good,
the youthful mother.
It was you I was searching for and did not think to find
within such easy reach
of all those, travellers
or exhausted woodsmen going by,
who seek for cover or for comfort.
Indeed, this shrine in whose presence I now stand,
gained with such uphill labour, offers itself
suddenly to the eye, dilapidated
(yet the only one whose jutting, tiny shed
could, in time of tempest, keep you dry),
to all who clamber up and cannot miss
its unwonted bulk among the other roadside shrines
encountered here and there, humbler
scored with prayers and childish insults.

But I must rejoice, not fall
into vain regrets, discovering that
this place of worship set apart, almost beyond my reach
who came here by the pathway of the dead,
guided by memory, the bitter privilege
of those too frugal with their joys,
fulfils its task, so readily and calmly
of protection for the body and the soul,
if one does not seek but finds it by the wayside,
open to all, though now without a name.

No one, I see, has brought up stones and lime
or fine sand from the clear banks
of the Bratica that flows below
through its long, deep earth-wound; no one
has put pack and saddle

ha imbastato il suo asino facendosi
precedere per il faticoso
itinerario dalla pazienza
della bestia, un giorno di lavoro
rubato alla cura del misero possesso,
nessuno di Casarola né per avventura
di Montebello equidistante, di sua
volontà o esortato dall'alto
di un pulpito mai stanco di pretendere,
ha restaurato questa che è, ancora,
la più bella maestà della montagna,
e lo fu, forse, per nostra vanità.
Ma, passando, uno ha impilato con ordine
pietre cadute dal muretto a secco
del recinto, un altro, o lo stesso, chi sa,
dimentico di sé nel quieto abbraccio
di questo portichetto di pace,
porto d'ombra,
ha sistemato sul tetto le sconnesse
piane d'ardesia in modo che almeno
non ci piova. E c'è sempre
qualche fiore o frutto, ma tanto
selvatico e stringente da stare
fra le dita rotte del bambino,
nello scollo adolescente
della madre.

Durerà, la costruzione boschiva,
fin che dura il dolore e la pietà
di chi abita ancora le terre alte
che noi abbandonammo.
E non è giusto il mio
batticuore violento, non è giusta
la mia scelta profanatoria
dell'ora della messa, per una
visita così privata, una devozione
solitaria, egoista come un vizio.
Datemi, sterpi e sassi, un passaggio
per liberarmi,
fate che io ritrovi una strada
battuta e aperta,
profumata dai cigli esposti a mattino

onto his ass and let it lead him
by that laborious track
it takes the patience of a beast
to follow – a day of labour
robbed from the concern
for a wretched patch of land; no one from Casarola, nor by chance
from equidistant Montebello, of his own free will
or exalted from the height
of a pulpit never tired of making claims
on others, has restored this one that is still
the most beautiful of mountain shrines
due, no doubt, to our vanity.
Yet, passing by this place someone has stacked
stones fallen from the drystone wall
enclosing it; another – the same, who knows? –
forgetful of self within the calm embrace
of this tiny portico of peace,
port of shade,
has put the slates to rights
that were sliding from its roof, so that at least
rain cannot enter. And always
there is some flower or fruit,
wild and shrivelled enough to fit
the broken fingers of the child,
the adolescent neckline
of the mother's dress.

It will last, this forest masonry,
as long as the pain and piety
of those who go on living on these heights
that we abandoned.
And the violence of my heartbeats
is not justified,
nor is my choice and profanation
of the hour of mass
for such a private visit, a devotion
solitary and selfish as a vice.
Scrub and stone, show me
a passage through to set me free,
and let me find once more
an open beaten track
perfumed from banks that catch the morning sun

per una moltitudine inebriante
di garofanini campestri
svegli presto e di già
un po' appassiti, eppure
lieti, senza memoria né speranza,
di un sole che sta
per lasciarli avanzando il meriggio
e tuttavia li riscalda e illumina ancora.

a heady multitude
of tiny wild carnations
wakened early, and already
wilting a little, though –
having neither memory nor hope –
blithe in the sunlight which will soon
leave them, as the afternoon draws on
and yet grant them warmth and illumination still.

NOTE: 'B' in the title stands for Bertolucci. The phrase
'due...to our vanity' refers also to that family.

Il tempo si consuma

Sono entrato nella gran folla mista
della messa di mezzogiorno, in cerca
di te, ch'eri là dall'inizio,
bambino diligente, anima pura
affamata di Dio, e con inquieto
occhio ho scrutato fra i banchi
inutilmente.
Ma da una tela umile veniva
incontro alla mia ansia il garzone
di falegname, Gesù, della tua età,
a rincuorarmi, mentre intorno, al fioco
accento del sacerdote lontano
si mescolava l'agitazione terrena
delle ragazze e dei ragazzi tenuti
lontani dal bel sole di domenica.
Così, d'improvviso, in un angolo vicino
alla porta, t'ho ritrovato, quieto
e solo, m'hai visto, ti sei
accostato timidamente, ho baciato
i tuoi capelli, figlio ritrovato
nel tempo doloroso che per me e te
e tutti noi con pena si consuma.

Time is Consuming Itself

I entered the great throng of young and old
at noonday mass, in search
of you, who were there from the beginning,
diligent child, pure soul
hungry for God, and with an unquiet eye
scrutinised the benches
fruitlessly.
But out of a humble canvas
advanced to meet my anxiety the carpenter's
apprentice, Jesus – his years were yours –
so as to encourage me, while all around
with the faint voice of the distant priest
mingled the worldly restlessness of girls and boys
kept from the Sunday sun too long.
Then, suddenly, by chance
in a corner by the door
a glance restored you to me
quiet and alone: you saw me too and timidly
drew near: I kissed you on the hair,
son found again
in a time of sorrow that for me and you
and all of us is consuming itself in pain.

Il giardino pubblico

In una torva luce
bambini e asinelli
consumano le ultime
ore del giorno, Dio

fa cessare quei loro
gesti dementi, manda
uno scroscio di pioggia
sulla pelle, sul pelo

affaticati e pesti
dal vivere e da ottobre
che madido si disfa,
e li trovi il crepuscolo

nelle stanze, le stalle
loro assegnate, quieti
e dispersi, e tu
che morendo li insanguini

e li redimi, o sole.

Public Garden

In a threatening light
children and donkeys
are wearing away the last
hours of day: Lord

put an end
to their frenzies, send
a shower of rain
on hide, on hair

tired out, worn down
by living and by October
damply dissolving;
and may twilight find them

in the rooms, the stalls
to which they are assigned,
quiet and dispersed, and you
who dying, blood-redden

and redeem them, sun.

Il vento e la pioggia

Perché oggi che il vento
porta cattivo tempo
i bambini nascosti
dalla tettoia azzurra di lamiera ondulata
infuriano sulla cagna malata, il gattino
occhidolci, è una femmina, porta
il topo in bocca come un figlio
prima di finirlo?
Questo vento che chiamano marino
cadrà e seguirà
una pioggia tiepida
e altri fatti mi addoloreranno. Poi
tornerà il sereno perché è estate
e venuta la notte
nei boschi neri di castagni gli essiccatoi
in rovina
risulteranno nuovi per la calcina della luna.

The Wind and the Rain

Why is it today when the wind
brings in bad weather
children hidden behind
a shed's blue corrugated iron
take out their tempers on a sick bitch, and the little cat
with soft-eyes – she's female – carries
the mouse in her mouth like a son
before finishing him off?
The wind they call a sea wind
will drop and there will follow
a tepid rain
with other things to grieve me. Then
clear skies will return because it's summer
and come the night
in the woods black with chestnuts the kilns for drying them
in ruins
will seem like new in the limewash of the moon.

Ritratto di uomo malato

Questo che vedete qui dipinto in sanguigna e nero
e che occupa intero il quadro spazioso
sono io all'età di quarantanove anni, ravvolto
in un'ampia vestaglia che mozza a metà le mani

come fossero fiori, non lascia vedere se il corpo
sia coricato o seduto: così è degli infermi
posti davanti a finestre che incorniciano il giorno,
un altro giorno concesso agli occhi stancantisi presto.

Ma se chiedo al pittore, mio figlio quattordicenne
chi ha voluto ritrarre, egli subito dice
'uno di quei poeti cinesi che mi hai fatto
leggere, mentre guarda fuori, una delle sue ultime ore.'

È sincero, ora ricordo d'avergli donato quel libro
che rallegra il cuore di riviere celesti
e brune foglie autunnali; in esso saggi, o finti saggi, poeti
graziosamente lasciano la vita alzando il bicchiere.

Sono io appartenente a un secolo che crede
di non mentire, a ravvisarmi in quell'uomo malato
mentendo a me stesso: e ne scrivo
per esorcizzare un male in cui credo e non credo.

Portrait of a Sick Man

This man you see here, portrayed in red and black
and who occupies the entire spacious picture
is me at the age of forty-nine wrapped up
in an ample dressing-gown that cuts the hands half off

as if they were flowers; you cannot tell whether the body
is lying down or is on a chair: it is like this with the sick
placed before windows framing the light of day –
another day doled out to eyes soon weary.

But when I ask the artist, my son of fourteen years,
whose portrayal he intended, he at once declares:
'One of those Chinese poets you had me read
as he gazes upon the world – in one of his last hours.'

What he says is true – now I remember giving him that book
which restores the heart with its celestial shores
and dark autumnal leaves: in it sages, or poets feigning sage
graciously take leave of life, their glasses raised.

Only I, who belong to a century that believes
it tells no lies, recognise in that sick man
myself lying to myself: and I take up my pen
to exorcise a sickness I do and do not believe in.

L'albergo

Qui fabbricano un albergo dove
la strada piega e io sento
l'odore di legno nuovo degli infissi odo
il suono dei carpentieri le voci intermittenti

prima di vedere la costruzione l'aria
dei mille metri è fresca a fine luglio
come d'autunno il castagno è malato
la sua doratura diffusa significa morte.

Mi dicono che le stanze da letto saranno cinque
le due più belle volte a tramontana
immagino estati che verranno in ombra
quasi perenne sino al dissanguarsi dei giorni.

Immagino dopo anni di esercizio inutili
strofinacci sul parquet rustico lenzuola
in acqua corrente di Bràtica al sole
fragrante delle nevi negli inverni a venire:

perché il vizio girovago sarà di qui transitato
godendo di queste lane e tele ed avrà
ripreso il suo andare vivacemente inquieto
lasciando impronte impossibili a togliersi.

Oh su di esse posare l'occhio indebolito e vorace
in un soggiorno preparato con cura
e disperazione trattando con gestori venuti
fra queste valli – dissestati – dalla pianura.

The Hotel

Here they are building a hotel where
the road bends and I can smell
the odour of new wood for the timber frames and hear
the sounds of the joiners the voices' intermittent swell

before I see the construction the air
at a thousand metres is as cool in late July
as in autumn the chestnut is sick
its scattered gold betokens death is near.

They tell me the bedrooms will be five in number
the two finest of them facing north
I can imagine summers when they'll stay
in almost perpetual shadow up to the very last day.

I can imagine after years of polishing useless
floorcloths on the rustic parquet some sheets
washed in running water from the Bratica hung in the sun
fragrant with the snows of winters that are yet to come:

for the wandering craze will have passed this way
having relished these blankets and this linen with almost love
off once more on its ceaselessly restless holiday
leaving imprints behind impossible to remove.

Oh for the weakened and voracious eye to light
on them in a stay that was planned with care
and desperation dealing with managers who came
into these valleys – and into debt – from the plain down there.

Eliot a dodici anni
(da una fotografia)

Oggi un vento caldo corre la terra,
non arido non secco come sarà più tardi,
trascinando foglie di rame in un suono
che imita l'inferno prepara il purgatorio

e la sua sonnolenza autunnale. Questo
è marzo con il sole che ti fa
stringere gli occhi fondi, brune violette
su cui s'aggrondano i capelli scomposti

quanto permette, o esige, l'etichetta della
Nuova Inghilterra esule su rive
meridionali: e tu mai di petto
vorrai combatterla. Vincerla –

se oggi l'amara bocca adolescente tale
proposito e impegno significa mentre
contro il muro di mattoni il fotografo
finge la tua esecuzione e i ginocchi

illanguidiscono colpevolmente al tepore
della stagione e dell'età – e vinta
abbandonarla vuota sulle rive del tempo,
e lucente, vorrà dire vivere e scrivere

sino al gennaio inclemente, all'inverno delle ossa.

Eliot at Twelve Years

(from a photograph)

Today a cold wind travels the earth,
not arid, parching as later it will be,
dragging down copper leaves with a sound
that imitates inferno, prepares purgatory

and its autumn somnolence. This
is March with a sun that forces you
to narrow your deep eyes, dark violets
over which your hair hangs untidily down

as far as is permitted or required
by a New England etiquette in exile
on southern shores: and you will never try
to combat it openly. To overcome it –

if today the bitter adolescent mouth
indicates such an aim and task while here
against a brick wall the photographer
feigns your execution and your knees

grow guiltily languid in the warmth
of the season and your youth – and once overcome
to leave it empty on the shores of time,
and shining, will mean to live and write

till inclement January, till the bones' own winter.

I mesi

(a Roberto Tassi)

Letto in Emile Mâle che gli scultori del Nord
nella serie dei mesi fanno trebbiatore settembre
in Italia fanno luglio.
Ma qui oltre i mille metri sull'Appennino non è

già il tempo girato un'altra volta l'estate sconfitta
e scesa in pianura come una villeggiante
stanca d'annuvolamenti meridiani?
Poi è tornato il sereno con lunghi respiri celesti

perché possano battere il grano maturato a fatica
con le more e le nocciole che ne limitano i campi
brevi e bruniti da piogge
rifugio di quaglie interrogantisi nel grigioazzurro

zinco dell'alba. Ora è il pomeriggio lento
a passare misurato al metronomo
del piccolo motore a scoppio
di una trebbiatrice in miniatura venuta dalla Toscanella

evoluta che sta dietro il crinale impervio e prende
tepore dal mare. Il cuore si rassicura e batte
regolare con la battitura
delle spighe se questa fatica o festa agricola dura

al chiudersi del millennio che s'apre con i mesi di Francia.

The Months
(to Roberto Tassi)

Read in Emile Mâle the fact that the sculptors of the North
in their series of months make September the thresher
in Italy they make July.
But here at a thousand metres and more in the Apennines

hasn't time already come round again with summer
beaten back and gone down to the plain
like a holidaymaker sick of cloudy noons?
Then clearness returns with respites long and blue

so that they can thresh the grain that ripened late
like the blackberries and hazelnuts that bound the space
of small rain-blackened fields
refuge of quails questioning one another in the grey-blue

zinc of dawn. Now it is afternoon and slow
to pass measured by the metronome
of the tiny engine
of a miniature thresher come from progressive Toscanella

that lies behind the forbidding ridge and gathers
warmth from the sea. One's heart grows calm again and beats
regularly with the beating
of the ears of wheat if this rural fatigue or feast can last

to the end of the millenium which opens with the months of France.

Ancora l'albergo

Non avevo mai visto delle pollastre bianche e azzurre
avvicinandomi mi avvidi che erano state dipinte
lo avevano fatto per distinguerle poi che le lasciavano libere
la tramontana estiva esilarava.

Dall'Appennino si vedevano le Alpi orlate di neve
la falce sibilando sull'erba alta e fresca minacciava
il cane bianco e nero che non si scostava
perché dove stava era il sole fiammante e il bucato

dell'albergo – dopo che tutti i clienti sono partiti
succede un silenzio così totale non ti meravigliare
della figlia-serva dodicenne infinitamente laboriosa –
suo è il compito arduo di levare le macchie

di trattenere il canto su la bocca bella piccola rosa.

The Hotel Once More

I had never seen chickens that were white and blue
getting closer I could tell that they'd been painted
it was done to distinguish them when let out to roam
the north wind of summer exhilarated you.

From the Apennines you saw the Alps outlined with snow
a scythe that hissed through the high cool grass was menacing
the black and white dog that refused to budge
because where he lay was blazing sun and the washing

from the inn – when not a guest remains
such a total silence follows you must not be surprised
by the twelve-year-old servant daughter hard at it and nothing loth –
hers is the arduous job to take out the stains

to keep back the song from her beautiful small rose mouth.

Frammento escluso dal romanzo in versi

«Angelica Kaufmann dipinse una scena
che io guardo riprodotta in un piatto
feriale, della prima colazione:
ha i colori un po' cancellati
dall'uso ma splendidi per il sole che vi batte
forte e libero alle nove del mattino d'estate
come un giovane di diciotto anni interamente virile.
Ma posso io che li compio a novembre
e non li anticipo ma mi ritraggo
felice di appartenere ancora alla pigra,
sudicia, irresponsabile adolescenza,
posso io, che medito su un piatto
ricavandone simboli personali,
contare sulla mia mattutina,
giovanile energia, sul suo
più diretto, naturale, utile impiego?
Quando poi m'identifico col putto
ebbro molle che poggia testa e schiena
sul grembo della donna di destra
e riceve una ghirlanda di grappoli viola
dalla donna a sinistra,
ronzando intorno una pianura assorta
in olmi anziani e folgorati, padri
attristati da una primavera perenne?
La circolarità del piatto mi dà
una vertigine cui non reggo, o è la nausea
per aver scoperto che il bambino
viene dalla madre ceduto in custodia
a un'estranea, e sia pure a una Musa?»

Fragment Left Out of the Novel in Verse

'It was Angelica Kaufmann who depicted
the scene before my eyes at breakfast-time
stamped on a plate for ordinary fare:
its colours are a little faded now
through use, but dazzle in a sun that beats
strong and free this summer's day at nine
like an eighteen-year-old virile to the core.
But can I, eighteen in November,
who do not look or wish to look my age,
still happy to identify myself
with an unwashed, lazy adolescence
in all its irresponsibility –
can I, in meditating on a plate,
deriving meanings that were made for me,
count on my morning, youthful energy
and on its most direct and natural use?
Above all when I actually feel
that drunk, effeminate boy and I are one,
resting his back and head upon the lap
of the woman on the right, whilst he receives
a garland from the woman on the left
of purple grapes, a humming plain all round
dreaming among its ancient blasted elms,
fathers saddened at perennial springtime here?
The circle of the plate has dizzied me
or is it nausea to find that child
yielded by his mother to the care
of a perfect stranger, even though a muse?

Solo

Di settembre qui arde ancora il sole
cero presso alla sua consumazione
il prato al quale accedo pianeggiante
è un altare la cui tovaglia è erbosa.

La trapungono colchici dall'incarnato lilla
l'orlano gli spini del Signore e di quella
maledetta proprietà che oggi è umiliata
dalla rovina lenta dell'agricoltura.

L'insanguinano le bacche in forte anticipo
sulla stagione autunnale l'addolciscono
il corallo vegetale della rosa canina
e il ciuffo tenace che stringe la nocciola.

Mi posso improvvisare prete – vocazione ritardata –
per celebrare nell'ora empia del mezzogiorno
su questa tavola naturale dell'appennino spazioso –
offrendo carne e sangue personali

agli asini alle lucertole alle farfalle in coppia
i soli che testimonino per i matronei disertati
la mia fede e la mia beatitudine inquieta –
mentre l'aereo postale si allontana e fila

una lana che nella distanza assolata scintilla?

Solo

In September here the sun burns on
a votive candle near to its consummation
the meadow I cross regaining level ground
is an altar whose cloth is one of grass.

Saffrons needle it through with their lilac incarnate
it is bordered by thorns of the Lord and by
those of that cursed landlust the times humiliate
beneath agriculture's slow decay.

Berries bloodstain it already in advance
of the autumn season a tenderness
shows in the coral hips of the dogrose
and the hardy tuft that tightens around the nut of the hazel.

Can I be preacher impromptu – a calling deferred –
to say mass at the impious noonday hour
on this natural table of spacious Apennine –
offering up this flesh and blood of mine

to the asses lizards butterflies in pairs
sole witnesses for the deserted benches where women pray
of my faith and my unquiet beatitude –
while the plane that carries the mail is drawing away and spins

a wool which in the distance spread out in sunlight scintillates?

LA CAMERA DE LETTO
THE BEDROOM
(1984, 1988)

1 *Fantasticando sulla migrazione dei maremmani*

Dalle maremme con cavalli, giorno
e notte, li accompagnavano nuvole
da quando partirono lasciandosi
dietro una pianura
e dietro la pianura il mare e l'orizzonte
in un fermo pallore d'alba estiva.
I cavalli erano svelti come nuvole
a rompere le gole, ad affacciarsi
alle valli. Ma ogni volta
che l'umido dei prati, il fragore
lontano d'un torrente, il soleggiato
ondulare d'una proda o altro segno
favorevole li tenne alti su un passo,
non tardò molto che l'occhio scoprì,
prima confuso all'azzurro dell'aria,
un fumo uscito lento dal mistero
d'un bosco di castagni e presto perso
alla vista già stanca,
già volta altrove, in cerca
d'un cammino più dolce per le bestie,
sospinte in là, dopo la sosta inutile,
e una così breve pastura. Le nuvole
non s'erano fermate, bisognava
andare avanti, era sempre appennino
profondo anche se altri
mandriani più miti già vi avevano
cresciuto agnelli e figli: non poteva
quell'infinito ondulare di valli
celesti nel silenzioso mezzogiorno
deluderli in eterno, mentre
il vento si placava, declinando
il giorno sui crinali in un calore
cui conveniva accucciarsi, cavando
pane e formaggio per la cena. Poi
venne un'ora limpidissima, l'ora
del pastore
che passa su ogni cima uno smeriglio
di luce solitaria; ma le valli
questa volta non echeggiarono del suono

1 *A History Imagined: the migration of the Maremmans*

From Maremma's fens with horses, day
and night clouds kept them company,
from their setting out leaving behind them
an open plain
and behind the plain the sea and the horizon
in the still pallor of the summer dawn.
The horses were as swift as clouds
breaking through gulleys, emerging
above the valleys. But every time
the moisture of meadows, the distant
roar of a torrent, the sun-caught undulation
of a bank or any other favourable sign
had kept them high above some mountain pass,
the eye was not slow to discover there,
confused first with the blueness of the air,
smoke rising slowly from the secrecy
of a wood of chestnuts and soon lost
to a gaze already wearied
turned already elsewhere, seeking
an easier pathway for the beasts,
goaded onwards after this useless pause
and so brief a pasture. The clouds
had made no halt, men too
must move on, for everywhere
bare mountainsides dropped sheer away
even though other and gentler herdsmen
had bred their sheep here and their sons: impossible
this infinite undulation of valleys
blue in the silence of the noon
should forever delude them, now
that the wind had dropped, the day
going down along the ridges in a warmth
agreeable to huddle in, to dig out
their meal of cheese and bread. Then
came the most limpid hour of all, the hour
of the shepherd
which burnishes each peak
with solitary light; but the valleys
this time did not echo with

cristiano che aiuta ad affrontare
la notte. Tante volte li aveva
rassicurati e respinti quel fioco
bronzo ad altre anime volto
che, il silenzio accrescendosi col buio,
un brivido li colse. O era la guazza
malefica alle ossa, che tra i faggi
li cacciò alla ricerca d'un tetto
di rami bassi, d'un letto di foglie,
per un sonno venuto tardi e andato
presto, nell'inquieta speranza?
I cavalli s'erano allontanati, il fratello
più giovane li trovò, abbeverati
e sazi, nella frescura d'un botro;
risalendo incontrò gli altri attorno
a un bel fuoco, dove a mezza costa
una radura pianeggiava, ardente
d'un mattino già caldo e d'una fiamma
domestica: un sito riparato
dai venti, ricco d'erba legna e acqua,
esposto al sole in modo conveniente.
Qui era tempo di fermarsi,
una terra per viverci, cavalli
e uomini, a lungo: forse l'arduo passo
che la sera li colse in dubbio, pena
e inconfessata speranza, aveva volto
altrove meno duri pastori
di questi che una piana aperta e molle
ma insidiata da febbre barattavano
con l'ignoto dell'alpe più scoscesa,
confabulando in pace attorno a un fuoco
spegnentesi, a due pietre annerite
e tiepide, a una cenere propizia.

that Christian sound which helps men to confront
the night. So many times
it had reassured them and repelled,
that faint bronze addressed to other souls,
so that now, silence thickening with the dark,
a shudder shook them. Or was it dew
that racked their bones and drove them
among the beech trees to seek out a roof
of low branches, a bed of leaves,
to snatch a sleep come late, soon lost
amid their unquiet hopes?
The horses had gone off, the youngest brother
found them again, sated and watered
in the shadowy coolness of a wide hollow;
climbing back out he found the others
at a good fire where half-way up the slope
a glade opened its level ground
bright with a day already warm
and with a homely blaze: a spot protected
against wind and rich in grass, wood, water,
let in what sun was needful and no more.
Here was the place and time to halt,
a land where horse and man might live
and live at length: perhaps the arduous pass
which had held them at day's end in doubt,
and fatigue and hope unspoken, had shown the way
elsewhere to shepherds of less hardy breed than these
who chose to exchange a soft and open plain
(though snared with fever)
for the unknown of the steepest alp,
conferring now in peace about a fire
extinguishing, between two blackened
and warm stones, into propitious ash.

X *Come nasce l'ansia*

A fine ottobre, se una sera il cielo
si addensa dopo il giorno più bello
dell'anno, la biancheria tutta asciutta
nei cesti il cui intreccio di fibre
giovani rompe di chiarore il buio
del tinello, nell'ora incerta prima
della lucerna accesa e della brace
ridestata, a tutti in casa viene
un pensiero della stagione che cambia.
Fuori c'è ancora qualcuno attardato,
un'ombra che ne incontra un'altra e tira
via o si ferma: gente del civile
e del rustico che la notte confonde
umanamente mentre cade tiepida
come lagrime una pioggia augurale
per semine da terminare
e sorgenti in via d'inaridirsi.

Così aveva inizio quell'inverno
che il bambino di Bernardo e Maria
compì cinque anni, il fratello più grande
in collegio. La pioggia
durò sino a Natale, salvo qualche
sosta e schiarita illusoria che vide
rilucere pozzanghere
attorno a casa, aggrupparsi passeri
sul marciapiede di mattoni rapido
ad asciugare scolorando in mite
rosa. Allora sarà venuto il tempo
di socchiudere con il cuore che batte forte
la porta a vetri incisi che mette
nel giardino abbandonato da tutti
fuori che dai suoi abitatori segreti,
da questa lumachina argentea di
bava che colpisce ora i tuoi occhi
disavvezzi alla luce di fuori
e li incanta così a lungo da fare
venir sera sopra il mondo abbrunato,
appena rotto a ovest da ferite

X *How Anxiety Is Born*

At October's end, if one evening the sky
clouds over after the loveliest day
of all the year, the washing dry
in the baskets of fresh fibre
whose weave glimmers against the darkness
of the breakfast room, in that uncertain hour
before the lighting of the lamp, the rousing of the embers,
there comes to everyone in the house
a thought of the season now about to change.
Outside a few still linger there,
a shadow that meets with another and
goes on its way or halts – the gentry
and country people that the night
sociably confuses with one another, while there falls
tepid as tears a rain
auspicious for the end of sowing
and for springs on the point of running dry.

This is how the winter began
when the child of Bernardo and Maria
completed his fifth year, his older brother
gone off to boarding school. The rain
lasted until Christmas, save for now and then
a pause, an illusory brightening that saw
a shine spread on the puddles
round the house, the sparrows gathering
on the path whose brickwork
was quick to dry, fading to a mild pink.
Then time must have come the moment
to set ajar with beating heart the door
with its patterned panes
giving onto the garden space abandoned
by all except its secret inhabitants,
by this tiny snail silvery with slime
which catches your eye now
unused to the outdoor light
and enchants it for so long that evening comes
over a darkened world
only broken in the west

lunghe di luce, lampi d'un lontano,
inconoscibile cielo che chiude
dietro di te la serva, infreddolita
e vivace, spingendoti nell'antro
familiare, pauroso oggi per troppe
ombre e troppi silenzi, sino a tardi.

Il rumore che tu credevi un trotto
avvicinantesi è di nuovo pioggia,
la delusione ti stringe all'istante
che tutta l'ansia accumulata stava
mutando in gioia come fa la nube
che s'illumina passando sul sole
e non è più quella che prima dava
un brivido alle ossa, ma un'altra
per cui la faccia ridendo traspira.
Come supereranno ora la notte
e il vento e l'acqua senza fine, come
le insidie che la strada degli argini
presenta proprio in quei gomiti cari
a chi cammina accaldato, primavera
o estate o primo autunno guernito
ancora di foglie di gaggìa,
Maria e Bernardo andati in città
per compere, avvicinandosi il tempo
delle feste che rallegrano il buio
di mezzo inverno con luci distanti.
Ora, al bambino in piedi su una sedia
accostata alla finestra, in tinello,
entra negli occhi, di là dalle sbarre
di pioggia un po' curvate dal vento,
un lume in movimento e per la china
che dal ponte del Cinghio scende nella
strada diretta agli Alberi – raccordo
da cui, fra due castagni d'India,
fugge il breve stradello padronale
che è principio e fine della vita – e
s'allontana.

La traballante, solitaria e fioca
cosa viaggiante prosegue il cammino
forse ancora lunghissimo, si stacca

by long wounds of light, flashes
in a far-off, inscrutable sky blotted out
behind you by the lively servant girl who feels the cold,
pushing you back into the familiar cavern,
fearful today with its too many shadows
and too many silences, until the evening.

The sound you took for a trot
coming towards you is once more rain;
the dismay gripped you at that instant
when all the store of your anxiety
was changing into joy just as the cloud
that lights up as it sails before the sun
is no longer that which earlier sent
a shudder through your bones, but one
that beads your smiling face with moisture.
How will they get the better of the night now
and the wind and the unending rain,
and all the lurking dangers the road along the dyke
confronts you with precisely on those sudden bends
dear to the walker toiling through the heat,
in spring or summer or the early autumn
the acacia still adorns with leaves,
Maria and Bernardo gone
to make their purchases in town, the time
now close at hand for those festivities which cheer
the darkness of midwinter with their distant lights.
Now, the child, standing on a chair
pushed to the window in the breakfast room,
catches from out beyond the bars
of falling rain slightly curving in the wind,
a moving gleam advancing down the slope
that drops from the Cinghio bridge
into the road for Gli Alberi – the junction
from where between the two horse-chestnut trees
runs the short private road
where his life begins and ends – but
it shrinks into the distance.

The unsteady, solitary and feeble
wandering thing pursues its way,
still very far perhaps, is gone

dalla pupilla febbrile, dal cuore
violento nella fragile armatura
che lo trattiene mentre egli quasi più
non sopporta l'attesa e si vorrebbe
perdere dietro la luce vagabonda
che s'allontana, maledetta: sono
gli zingari che rubano i bambini,
li raccolgono se sono fuggiti
di casa? Ora lo stoppino fila
fiamma rossastra e fumo dentro il tubo
della lucerna, hai voltato le spalle
alla finestra per cercare requie
nella stanza prostrata dalla brace,
smangiata nei muri dall'ombra, fulgente
nel mezzo per la tovaglia che accresce,
non placa l'ansia cui cerchi rimedio
configgendo nella falange puerile
l'unghia debole bianca di bugìe.

Fila intanto la pendola i secondi,
insonne dispensatrice di un tempo
di tremiti che ti sfama lasciandoti
sazio sino alla nausea davanti
al dolce cibo delle guance umide
e fresche di Maria ritornata
senza che tu abbia udito alla pioggia
mischiarsi il trotto smorente,
per cessare nell'alone allegro
della lucerna, riverberata di fuori
come un saluto quieto a chi di nuovo
si trova qui, dove voleva, in pace.
Maria non si è accorta della tua
piccola ripulsa, del tuo imbarazzo
nel ricambiare l'abbraccio, ti ha
lasciato ancora solo, è andata
a nascondere i doni, a occuparsi
della cena: chiudi gli occhi perduto
in una spossatezza senza fine,
convalescente che gode il suo stato
come un peccato o come un privilegio.

from his own burning pupil, from his heart
violent within the fragile armature
that restrains it still while the waiting
so much weighs on him he'd rather choose
to lose himself behind the roaming light
that, fatefully, moves on: can it be
the gypsies who steal children
or give them shelter if they
run away from home? Now the wick
smokes in a reddish flame inside the chimney
of the lamp; you have turned your back
on the window to find comfort
in the room dejected by its embers,
its walls eaten away by shadow, shining
at its centre with the tablecloth which increases
and does not pacify the anxiety you seek to quell,
clenching into the joints of childish fingers
weak nails whose spots of white betoken lies.

The pendulum all the while counts out the seconds,
insomniac dispenser of a time
of tremblings which satiate and which leave you
glutted with nausea when you see
the sweet food of the moist, fresh cheeks
of Maria who has come back home
without your having heard beneath the rain
the fading trot, that ceased in the cheerful halo
of the lamp thrown back outside
like a quiet greeting meant for those
who find themselves here once more
where they wished to be, and safe.
Maria was not aware
of your brief rejection, of your embarrassment
in responding to her hug; she has
left you alone again, has gone
to hide the presents, to busy herself
with supper: you close your eyes
lost in a lassitude without end,
a convalescent who enjoys his state,
like a transgression or a privilege.

XXIII *O Salmista*

Don Attilio

Emma, la fronte ai vetri di chi medita dolori,
in questo mezzogiorno di primavera montana veglia
don Attilio, che è ancora vivo, dietro le sue spalle,
ma muore, non fa altro da mesi, da anni,
che morire. Eppure è possibile a lei ancora
di quest'uomo folgorato, stroncato, atterrato,
rinarrarsi lunghe stagioni attive
e felici, fumi d'altare e di cucina, incenso e caffè
confondendosi da chiesa a canonica, e viceversa,
in corridoi umidi invasi da gente stordita,
allegre per le festività cattoliche in cui è bello
potersi immergere mani intrecciate e cuori in fretta
palpitanti per nozze battesimi cresime, argenti
sfolgorando anche nelle ammaccature e nelle pezze chiodate,
rose spargendo perdizione sensuale
in questo permesso, benedetto paganesimo della nostra
religione. E aggiungi per lui il peccato (veniale)
della poesia rinvigorita dall'innesto modernista
ma illanguidita dalla luce di perdizione delle cupole parmigiane.

XXIII *O Psalmist*

Don Attilio

Emma, pressing against the panes
the forehead of one meditating sorrows,
this midday of mountain spring
watches beside the bed of Don Attilio
who, behind her back, is still alive
yet dying – has done nothing for months, for years
but die. Yet it is possible even now for her
thinking of this paralysed, felled, broken man,
to re-live in memory long seasons
active and happy, fumes from altar and from kitchen,
incense and coffee mingling together
between church and rectory, and back again;
in damp passage-ways invaded by a gaping throng,
times gladdened by those catholic festivities in which
it is so lovely to immerse oneself, clasped hands and hearts in haste
throbbing at marriages, christenings, confirmations, silver
blazing even in its dints and rivets,
roses scattering sensual perdition
in this permitted, blessed paganism which is our
religion. And add for him the sin (venial merely)
of poetry invigorated by the graft
of modernism and then softened by
the light of perdition from the domes of Parma.

XXXI *Le Scarpette di chevreau*

In tempi di anglofobìa ufficiale
l'anglofilìa dà piaceri sottili. A.
e il suo amico Virginio hanno scoperto
nel magazzino che rappresenta
per l'Italia Burberry, Allen Solly, Lock,
un baule di campionario invecchiato
da cedere per pochi centesimi
allo straccivendolo che intona la sua voce,
stonata tromba, per i borghi
di Parma sorridenti
a una primavera precoce, azzurra e bianca,
bruna soltanto nell'ondulazione dei coppi.
I due giovani oziosi, è quasi mezzogiorno,
frugando senza requie riportano alla luce
meraviglie di lane sete e cuoi intatti,
colori che dovevano lottare con la nebbia
mentre ora gareggiano con la luce italiana
nel colpire gli occhi, nell'incantarli
con i loro accostamenti qualche volta
inattesi, come nel verde e blu
d'una reggimentale che i tagli della seta
nobilitano quasi ferite di guerra.
A un certo punto Virginio si stupisce
nel vedere il suo compagno in questa
avventura di riscoperte labili,
in questo divertimento, brillare
negli occhi di una gioia più intensa,
quasi dolorosa: tiene le mani
immerse in due scarpette femminili
di tenera pelle verde, dai lacci
così lunghi che s'immagina debbano
stringere la caviglia in una guisa
desueta oggi, ma forse...A. è preso
da un piccolo batticuore, confusamente
temendo che il numero non sia quello giusto,
che forse N... No, non può non donargliele,
oltre al fatto di non essere alla moda,
pregio in più, aggiungi il gusto di un'Inghilterra
in cui ragazze a nome Katherine, Virginia,

XXXI *The Doeskin Shoes*

In times of official anglophobia
subtle are the joys of anglophilia. A.
and his friend Virginio have discovered
at the warehouse that represents
Burberry, Allen Solly, Lock, in Italy,
a trunk of antiquated samples,
to be exchanged for only a few pence
with the rag and bone man who,
his voice like a trumpet out of tune,
strikes up through the outskirts of Parma
smiling at early springtime, blue and white,
brown only in the undulation of the tiles.
The two idle youths – it is almost midday –
rummaging endlessly bring to light
marvels in wool, silk, leather
all intact, in colours
that had to struggle with the fog
and now compete with the Italian light
to catch the eye, enchant it,
with unexpected juxtaposings
as in the green and blue of regimentals
dignified like old war wounds
by the fine cut of the silks.
At a certain point Virginio is amazed
to see his companion in this short-lived
treasure-hunt, in this diversion,
has eyes shining with an even more intense,
an almost painful joy: his hands are thrust
inside two dainty lady's shoes
of soft green leather, with the laces
so long that he imagines them designed
to be drawn tight around the ankle in a mode
now out of fashion, but perhaps... A. begins to feel
a quickening of his heartbeat, vaguely
fearing the size will not be right,
that perhaps N... No, he cannot not give them to her,
aside from the fact of their outmoded style,
an extra merit, they reflect the taste of an England
in which girls called Katherine, Virginia

avevano potuto calzare
coturni così leggeri, del colore dell'erba...
Le porta già, anche se le sono un po' lunghe,
un po' vuote in punta.
Da sentirsi dire: «Nei piedi sembri Greta Garbo.» «Non mi dispiace.»
Ma vuole che A. l'accompagni da Gelasio
che fa scarpe su misura. È un timido,
fine artigiano, venuto da poco in città
da Basilicanova, terra di dialetto femmineo, cantante.
«In altra pelle, se questa verde
non è possibile trovarla da nessuna parte.»
Lui consiglia un *chevreau* marrone
come quello che ha tanto accontentato
A.: avranno scarpe dello stesso cuoio,
e a lui questo dà una sorta di nuova ebbrezza.
E i lacci li fabbricherà lui, terminanti
in quel grazioso frastaglio. Erano anni
che non ne faceva più, perché non li vuole
nessuno...«ma se i signorini li gradiscono, saranno
accontentati». Nell'odore della pece
e dei pellami s'insinua aria di fuori,
a folate, dai finestrini aperti
dello scantinato, e chiama
a un mattino di sole da attraversare insieme.

[......]

Oggi, sabato mattina, A. e N.
si sono dati appuntamento a un bar
che sta sul lungoparma e possiede
una pergola alta, verdeggiante.
Lui cerca,
trova i tavolini deserti, considera
l'umidità notturna sulle sedie di ferro.
Significa, ciò, che è ancora presto, non bisogna
pretendere che una ragazza sia svelta
nello svegliarsi e approntarsi ad uscire:
lui sa che i soprassalti le procurano
una cefalea dura ad andarsene
senza l'aiuto del véramon. Poi
ci sarà stato il tè preparato dalla mamma,
un po' forte, all'uso australiano...

might well have worn such buskins
as light as ballet shoes, the colour of grass...
In no time she is wearing them, although
a little long, a little empty at the toe.
People might say: 'Your feet look like Greta Garbo.'
She: 'I don't mind that.'
But she wants him to accompany her
to Gelasio who makes shoes to measure. He is a shy
sensitive craftsman, newly arrived in town
from Basilicanova, home of a lilting feminine dialect.
'In a different skin, if this green one
cannot be found somewhere.'
He recommends a brown *chevreau*,
of the sort A. was already so much taken by:
they will both have shoes of the same leather,
and this thought brings on a sort of new inebriation.
And the laces he will make himself,
ending in that graceful fringe. It is years
since he made any of that kind
because nobody wants them...'But if the young lady and gentleman
so wish, I shall be glad to oblige.' The outside air
mingles with the smell of pitch and hides
in gusts through the open basement windows, summoning them
to a morning of sun to walk through together.

[......]

Today, Saturday morning, A. and N.
have arranged to meet at a bar
on the street along the river, which possesses
a high leafy pergola.
He gazes round,
finds the tables are deserted, contemplates
the dampness of the night on the iron chairs.
Which means that it's still early: one shouldn't expect
a girl to be quick in waking up
and getting ready to go out:
he knows that any undue haste
gives her a headache, hard to get rid of
without the help of Véramon. Then
there comes tea, prepared by her mother,
rather strong, in the Australian way...

Poco altro, non è tipo da *toilettes* interminabili:
si capisce che il lavarsi, il pettinarsi,
l'aggiungere rosso alle guance brune (questo artificio
che lui ama), vogliono un certo tempo. Mentre
tali riflessioni volge dentro di sé,
più ansioso che impaziente, gli è
entrata nell'occhio senza accorgersi
di lui, in modo che la può vedere
alerte alla destinazione immancabile,
che è lui. È geloso
e innamorato della solitudine fiera
del suo portamento
che dà ardore all'aria mattutina,
compiutezza alla giornata celeste,
tesa sui ponti di Parma e l'acqua primaverile
come una tela calma...

Gelasio non è solo, sembra
arrossire quando entrano,
e con la sua vocina deve pregarli
di accomodarsi un momento. Il cliente,
che sta piegato sul panchetto,
non sembra accorgersi di loro: difficile
stabilire che cosa faccia
perché non parla e muove appena il braccio destro
mentre Gelasio torna a lui;
A. lo osserva con minuta attenzione. L'abito
un po' cascante della giacca che veste
con trascuratezza una schiena lunga e curva,
si rivela di alta qualità: una grisaglia
anche troppo leggera per la stagione.
Ha finito,
ora si capisce, mentre alza il foglio che disegnava,
e contemporaneamente solleva le grandi
membra stanche di uomo non più giovane.
Parla con voce alta,
nobile nella sua durezza e tentata
urbanità: raccomanda il tacco
con una nuova, maniacale espressione.
Per la prova va bene quest'altro sabato?
Gelasio l'accompagna alla porta vetrata,
lo lascia allontanare terribilmente solo

Not much else, she doesn't go in for interminable *toilettes*:
Naturally, washing herself and doing her hair,
adding a little red to her dark cheeks (that artifice
he is so fond of), must take a certain time. While
he is ruminating in this way
more anxious than impatient, she enters his line of vision
without being aware of him,
so that he is able to catch sight of her
alert for the unfailing destination
which is himself. He is envious
and in love with the proud solitude
of the way she holds herself
which gives warmth to the morning air,
completeness to the heavenly day,
spread out above the bridges of Parma and its vernal waters
like a calm painted canvas...

Gelasio is not alone, he seems
to blush when they enter,
and in his small voice he asks them
would they wait a moment. The customer
who is bending over the workbench
seems unaware of them: difficult
to know exactly what he is at
since he does not speak and moves his right arm
only slightly as Gelasio returns to him;
A. observes him with minute attention. The jacket
of his suit, hanging loosely on him,
negligently clothing a long curved back,
declares its high quality: a greyish cloth
rather too lightweight for the season.
He is finished:
now one understands, as he raises the sheet that he was drawing on,
and at the selfsame moment lifts the large
tired limbs of a man no longer young.
He speaks in a lofty voice,
noble in its severity and willed urbaneness,
and commends the heel
with an odd, maniacal expression.
For the trying on, next Saturday?
Gelasio accompanies him to the glass door,
leaving him to walk away, terribly alone,

nella vivace folla del borgo parmigiano.
Non c'è bisogno che A. chieda, mentre
N. calza sulle bemberg lucide e chiare
le scarpe che calzano a pennello,
e Gelasio ha troppo bisogno di sfogarsi
per stare zitto. Sì, è il suo
cliente migliore, ma se sapessero...
Disegna lui i modelli, procura lui pelli introvabili a Parma,
è esigente
come se dovesse portarle lui... No,
sono per la signora che viene soltanto
a provarle, e non parla mai. Più giovane?
Non si direbbe, bella, molto alta,
come lui, s'assomigliano,
non parlano fra loro, mai,
sono dei genovesi.
I genovesi sono gente strana, questi,
gran signori, abitano una villa
in collina, di primavera, e d'autunno molto a lungo,
forse per la caccia, Hanno tanta terra
in provincia, e tanta ne hanno
altri, loro parenti e amici, anche
nel piacentino...N. è felice,
le stanno così bene. Ma quando
escono, lei e A., salutato Gelasio,
si guardano con un'espressione grave
negli occhi amorosi. È come se
in questa mattina tiepida
fossero stati investiti
da folate di aria fredda, e ora
penassero a scaldarsi nuovamente.

into the animated crowd at this end of town.
A. has no need to ask
as N. draws on over clear shining stockings
the shoes that fit her to perfection –
and Gelasio needs too much to let himself go
to stay silent. Yes, it is his
best customer, but if only they knew...
He draws the patterns himself; he gets hides
you would never find in Parma; he is hard to please
as if he himself were going to wear them... No,
they are for his wife who only comes
to try them on, and never speaks. Younger?
Not really – good-looking, very tall
like him, they resemble each other,
they do not exchange a word though, never:
they are Genoese.
The Genoese are strange people – these,
real upper crust, live at a villa
in the hills, in spring, and then almost all the autumn
perhaps because of the shooting. They've a lot of land
in the provinces, their friends and relatives
own a whole lot more as far afield
as Piacenza... N. is happy:
they fit her to perfection. But when
(with farewells to Genasio) they leave,
she and A. gaze at each other with a grave expression
in their loving eyes. It is as if
on this mild morning
they had come into collision
with cold gusts of air, and now
were finding it difficult to warm themselves again.

VERSO LE SORGENTI DEL CINGHIO

TOWARDS THE SOURCES OF THE CINGHIO

(1993)

Giovanni Diodati

(a Charles Tomlinson)

La mia meraviglia quasi felicità
quando ho scoperto che Giovanni Diodati –
del quale leggevo la Bibbia protestante
chissà come finita nella mia casa cattolica –

tiepida negli obblighi ma di radici tenaci –
era amico di quel John Milton
che oggi – tardi – conto fra i poeti
da me più amati...Il cangiante

dei suoi versi se dipinge Eva nuda
guarnire una tovaglia
di rosseggianti pomi nell'autunno
del Paradiso corruscando il meriggio

all'avvicinarsi dell'ospite –
Raffaele Arcangelo – per un pranzo a tre –
non è quale nella prosa dell'esule
sulle rive del Lago Lemàno

svela la Sposa del Cantico
suggerendo al lettore adolescente –
crepuscoli entrando obliqui
nel granaio sonoro di frumento
nascondiglio aereo vertigine della mente
su una pianura nera di rondini –
la saliva dei baci?

Giovanni Diodati
(to Charles Tomlinson)

My astonishment almost felicity
when I discovered that Giovanni Diodati
whose protestant Bible I used to read –
who knows how it ended up in my Catholic household

tepid in observance but with tenacious roots –
was the friend of that John Milton
whom today – late – I count among those poets
I care for most. The shimmer

of his lines if he depicts Eve naked
garnishing a cloth
with reddening apples in the autumn
of Paradise its noonday corruscating

at the guest's approach –
Archangel Raphael – for a meal for three –
isn't it the same when in the prose of the exile
on the shores of Lake Leman

the Bride of the Canticle unveils
suggesting to the intent adolescent –
fiery twilights coming slantwise in
to the granary resonant with wheat
hiding-place in air vertigo of the mind
above a plain black with swallows – the saliva of kisses?

The Coastguard's House

EUGENIO MONTALE

English versions by Jeremy Reed

ITALIAN-ENGLISH BILINGUAL EDITION

POETRY BOOK SOCIETY TRANSLATION AWARD

'Eugenio Montale is the greatest Italian poet of the 20th century. Born in Genoa in 1889, he achieved sudden fame during the 1920s when his pessimistic poetry caught the mood of Italy in the culturally sterile years following the First World War. His stoical outlook echoed T.S. Eliot's, whose work he translated, but the source of much of his imagery was the barren, rocky landscape of his native Liguria – transmuted in his poems into an almost mythical setting. He won the Nobel Prize for Literature in 1975, and died in 1981.

'Spontaneous naturalness...the product of that exquisite and sure tact which is consummate art...Montale is as truly sophisticated as a major artist can be. That sophistication is apparent in the wit, irony and humour that intensify the effect of profound seriousness characterising the poetry...We have nothing like it in English'
– F.R. LEAVIS

'It was Robert Lowell's freedom in handling his *Imitations* and the dynamic lift he gave to the originals which convinced me that a version rather than a strict translation would prove more valuable to the English reader. In these versions I have tried to create the poem in English which Montale might have written in the last decade of the 20th century. I think the future of translation lies in this: the extension of two sensibilities to create a poetry which otherwise would not have existed' – JEREMY REED

Jeremy Reed has been described by David Gascoyne as 'the most outstanding poet of his generation'. His latest books are *Selected Poems* (Penguin, 1987), *Engaging Form* (Cape, 1989) and *Nineties* (Cape, 1990). He lives in London.

Italian Landscape Poems
Translated by Alistair Elliot

ITALIAN-ENGLISH BILINGUAL EDITION

This fascinating book isn't just a gathering of brilliant poems by some of Italy's finest writers. It explores attitudes to landscape, and what Italians call their *paese*, meaning both 'my town, my village, the countryside I come from' as well as the country as a whole. It's about liking a hill-walk (Leopardi) or hating the loneliness of country places (Belli); about landscape as sex-object (Ariosto) or moral stage-set (Tasso), as a place for visions (D'Annunzio) or nostalgia (Pascoli); about a spring that recalls national history (Carducci) and a holy place that reminds us foreigners are human too (Giusti).

Through poems or excerpts from the greatest Italian poems, this tragical-comical-historical-pastoral book presents a view of Europe's changing attitudes to the stuff under all our feet, from the bright and traditional Middle Ages into this gloomy and personal century. The poems, chosen by Alistair Elliot, are printed opposite his translations. There are also helpful notes on Italian verse technique and on points of obscurity.

This is Alistair Elliot's fourth book of verse translation – the others being Verlaine's *Femmes/Hombres* (Anvil), Heine's *The Lazarus Poems* (MidNAG/Carcanet) and *French Love Poems* (Bloodaxe, 1991). He has also edited a parallel-text edition of Virgil's *Georgics* with Dryden's translation (MidNAG), and translated Euripides' *Medea*, the basis of Diana Rigg's prize-winning performance at the Almeida Theatre (1992). Alistair Elliot's own Collected Poems, *My Country* (1989), and his latest collection, *Turning the Stones* (1993), are published by Carcanet.

Bloodaxe Contemporary French Poets

Series Editors: Timothy Mathews & Michael Worton

FRENCH-ENGLISH BILINGUAL EDITIONS

1: **Yves Bonnefoy:** *On the Motion and Immobility of Douve / Du mouvement et de l'immobilité de Douve*
Translated by Galway Kinnell. Introduction by Timothy Mathews.

2: **René Char:** *The Dawn Breakers / Les Matinaux*
Translated & introduced by Michael Worton.

3: **Henri Michaux:** *Spaced, Displaced / Déplacements Dégagements*
Translated by David & Helen Constantine. Introduction by Peter Broome.

FORTHCOMING:

4: **Aimé Césaire:** *Notebook of a Return to My Native Land / Cahier d'un retour au pays natal*
Translated by Mireille Rosello & Annie Pritchard.
Introduction by Mireille Rosello.

5: **Philippe Jaccottet:** *Under Clouded Skies / Beauregard Pensées sous les nuages / Beauregard*
Translated by David Constantine & Mark Treharne.
Introduction by Mark Treharne.

6: **Anne Hébert:** *The Tomb of the Kings / Le tombeau des rois*
Translated by Joanne Collie & Anne Hébert.
Introduction by Joanne Collie.

7: **Paul Éluard:** *Poésie ininterrompue II / Uninterrupted Poem II*
Translated by Gilbert Bowen.
Introduction by Jill Lewis.

Other books planned for the series include works by Jacques Dupin, André Frénaud, Guillevic, Pierre-Jean Jouve, Gérard Macé.

BLOODAXE CONTEMPORARY FRENCH POETS: 1
YVES BONNEFOY
On the Motion and Immobility of Douve:
Du mouvement et de l'immobilité de Douve
Translated by Galway Kinnell. Introduction by Timothy Mathews.

Yves Bonnefoy is a central figure in post-war French culture. Born in 1923, he has had a lifelong fascination with the problems of translation. Language, for him, is a visceral, intensely material element in our existence, and yet the abstract quality of words distorts the immediate, material quality of our contact with the world.

This concern with what separates words from an essential truth hidden in objects involves him in wide-ranging philosophical and theological investigations of the spiritual and the sacred. But for all his intellectual drive and rigour, Bonnefoy's poetry is essentially of the concrete and the tangible, and addresses itself to our most familiar and intimate experiences of objects and of each other.

In his first book of poetry, published in France in 1953, Bonnefoy reflects on the value and mechanism of language in a series of short variations on the life and death of a much loved woman, Douve. In his introduction, Timothy Mathews shows how Bonnefoy's poetics are enmeshed with his philosophical, religious and critical thought.

Galway Kinnell is one of America's leading poets. His *Selected Poems* (1982) won the National Book Award and the Pulitzer Prize.

BLOODAXE CONTEMPORARY FRENCH POETS: 2

RENÉ CHAR
The Dawn Breakers:
Les Matinaux
Edited & translated by Michael Worton

René Char (1907-88) is generally regarded as one of the most important modern French poets. Admired by Heidegger for the profundity of his poetic philosophy, he was also a hero of the French Resistance and in the 1960s a militant anti-nuclear protester.

Associated with the Surrealist movement for several years and a close friend of many painters – notably Braque, Giacometti and Picasso – he wrote poetry which miraculously, often challengingly, confronts the major 20th century moral, political and artistic concerns with a simplicity of vision and expression that owes much to the poet-philosophers of ancient Greece.

Les Matinaux (1947-49) is perhaps his greatest collection. Published after the War, it looks forward to a better and freer world, whilst also bearing the marks of a deep-seated hatred of all fascisms. It contains some of the most beautiful love poems ever written in French.

Michael Worton's translations convey the essence of Char's poetry (which says difficult things in a simple, traditional way), and his introduction suggests why Char is one of the vital voices of our age.

HENRI MICHAUX

Spaced, Displaced:
Déplacements Dégagements

Translated by David & Helen Constantine. Introduction by Peter Broome.

Henri Michaux (1899-1984) is one of the notable travellers of modern French poetry: not only to the Amazon and the Far East, but into the strange hinterland of his own inner space, the surprises and shocks of which he has never ceased to explore as a foreign country in their own right, and a language to be learned. Fired by the same explorer's appetite, he has delved into the realm of mescaline and other drugs, and his wartime poetry, part of a private "resistance" movement of extraordinary density and energy, has advertised his view of the poetic act as a form of exorcism.

His insatiable thirst for new artistic expressions of himself made him one of the most aggressive and disquieting of contemporary French painters. If he is close to anyone, it is to Klee and Pollock, but he was as much inspired by Oriental graphic arts.

Déplacements Dégagements (1985) has all the hallmarks of Michaux's most dynamic work: poetry testing itself dangerously at the frontiers, acutely analytical, linguistically versatile and full of surprising insights into previously undiscovered movements of the mind.

David Constantine is Fellow in German at the Queen's College, Oxford. He has published four books of poems and a novel with Bloodaxe, and has translated poetry from French, Greek and German. **Helen Constantine** has taught French at schools and polytechnics in Durham and Oxford. **Peter Broome** is Reader in French at Queen's University, Belfast. He is co-author of *The Appreciation of Modern French Poetry* and *An Anthology of Modern French Poetry* (CUP, 1976), and author of monographs on Michaux and Frénaud.

Other French Editions from Bloodaxe

JACQUES DUPIN
Selected Poems
Translated by Paul Auster, Stephen Romer & David Shapiro

Jacques Dupin was born in 1927 in Privas in the Ardèche. Images of the harsh mineral nakedness of his native countryside run through the whole of his work and figure a fundamental existential nakedness. Dupin is an ascetic who likes the bare and the simple. His poetry is sad, wise and relentlessly honest. He speaks in our ear, as if at once close and far off, to tell us what we knew: 'Neither passion nor possession'.

He is a poet and art critic, and a formidable authority on the work of Miró and Giacometti. This edition of his prose poems and lyrics has been selected by Paul Auster from seven collections published between 1958 and 1982, culminating in his *Songs of Rescue*. It has an introduction by Mary Ann Caws, Professor of French at City University of New York.

PIERRE REVERDY
Selected Poems
Translated by John Ashbery, Mary Ann Caws & Patricia Terry
Edited by Timothy Bent & Germaine Brée

Pierre Reverdy (1889-1960) is one of the greatest and most influential figures in modern French poetry. He founded the journal *Nord-Sud* with Max Jacob and Guillaume Apollinaire, which drew together the first Surrealists. Associated with painters such as Picasso, Gris and Braque, he has been called a Cubist poet, for conventional structure is eliminated in his *poésie brut* ('raw poetry'), much as the painters cut away surface appearance to bring through the underlying forms. But Reverdy went beyond Cubist desolation to express a profound spiritual doubt and his sense of a mystery in the universe forever beyond his understanding.

André Breton hailed him in the first Surrealist Manifesto as 'the greatest poet of the time'. Louis Aragon said that for Breton, Soupault, Éluard and himself, Reverdy was 'our immediate elder, the exemplary poet'.

JEAN TARDIEU
The River Underground:
Selected Poems & Prose
Translated by David Kelley

Jean Tardieu's poetry has an almost child-like simplicity, and in France his work is studied both in universities and in primary schools. Yet while he is a household name in France and has been translated into most European languages, his poetry remains little known in the English-speaking world, despite its immediacy and sense of fun.

Tardieu was born in 1903, and this selection spans 80 years of his writing. In his early years the difficulties of writing lyric poetry in a schizophrenic age led him to a multiplication of poetic voices, and so to working for the stage, and he was writing what was subsequently dubbed 'Theatre of the Absurd' before Beckett's and Ionesco's plays had ever been performed.

This selection includes the sequence *Space and the Flute* (1958), which Tardieu wrote for drawings by his friend Pablo Picasso. Their poems and drawings are reproduced together in this edition.

ALISTAIR ELLIOT
French Love Poems
Poetry Book Society Recommended Translation

French Love Poems is about the kinds of love that puzzle, delight and afflict us throughout our lives, from going on walks with an attractive cousin before Sunday dinner (Nerval) to indulging a granddaughter (Hugo). On the way there's the first yes from lips we love (Verlaine), a sky full of stars reflected fatally in Cleopatra's eyes (Heredia), lying awake waiting for your lover (Valéry), and the defeated toys of dead children (Gautier).

The selection covers five centuries, from Ronsard to Valéry. Other poets represented include Baudelaire, Mallarmé, Rimbaud, La Fontaine, Laforgue and Leconte de Lisle. The 35 poems, chosen by Alistair Elliot, are printed opposite his own highly skilful verse translations. There are also helpful notes on French verse technique and on points of obscurity.